William Somerville

The Chace

A poem

William Somerville

The Chace
A poem

ISBN/EAN: 9783744718349

Printed in Europe, USA, Canada, Australia, Japan

Cover: Foto ©Thomas Meinert / pixelio.de

More available books at **www.hansebooks.com**

THE

C H A C E.

A

P O E M.

By WILLIAM SOMERVILE, Esq.

Nec tibi cura canum fuerit postrema.
VIRG. GEORG. III.

Romanis solenne viris opus, utile famæ,
Vitæque, et membris.
HOR. EP. XVIII. Lib. I.

THE SIXTH EDITION.

LONDON:
Printed for W. BOWYER, W. STRAHAN,
and R. BALDWIN. MDCCLXXIII.

THE

PREFACE.

THE old and infirm have at leaſt this privilege, that they can recal to their minds thoſe ſcenes of joy in which they once delighted, and ruminate over their paſt pleaſures, with a ſatisfaction almoſt equal to the firſt enjoyment. For thoſe ideas, to which any agreeable ſenſation is annexed, are eaſily excited; as leaving behind the moſt ſtrong and permanent impreſſions. The amuſements of our youth are the boaſt and comfort of our declining years. The ancients carried this notion even yet further, and ſuppoſed their heroes in the Elyſian Fields were fond of the very ſame diverſions they exerciſed on earth. Death itſelf could not wean them from the accuſtomed ſports and gayeties of life.

Pars in gramineis exercent membra palæſtris,
Contendunt ludo, et fulvâ luctantur arenâ:
Pars pedibus plaudunt choreas, et carmina dicunt.
Arma procul curruſque virûm miratur inanes.

Stant

Stant terrâ defixæ haſtæ, paſſimque ſoluti
Per campos paſcuntur equi. Quæ gratia currûm
Armorumque fuit vivis, quæ cura nitentes
Paſcere equos, eadem ſequitur tellure repôſtos.

VIRG. Æneid. VI.

Part on the graſſy cirque their pliant limbs
In wreſtling exerciſe, or on the ſands
Struggling diſpute the prize. Part lead the ring,
Or ſwell the chorus with alternate lays.
The chief their arms admires, their empty cars,
Their lances fix'd in earth. Th' unharneſs'd ſteeds
Graze unreſtrain'd; horſes, and cars, and arms,
All the ſame fond deſires, and pleaſing cares,
Still haunt their ſhades, and after death ſurvive.

I hope therefore I may be indulged (even by the more grave and cenſorious part of mankind) if at my leiſure hours, I run over, in my elbow-chair, ſome of thoſe chaces, which were once the delight of a more vigorous age. It is an entertaining, and (as I conceive) a very innocent amuſement. The reſult of theſe rambling imaginations will be found in the following poem; which if equally diverting to my readers, as to myſelf, I ſhall have gained my end. I have intermixed the preceptive parts with ſo many deſcriptions and digreſſions in the Georgick manner, that I hope they will not be tedious. I am ſure they

they are very neceſſary to be well underſtood by any gentleman, who would enjoy this noble ſport in full perfection. In this at leaſt I may comfort myſelf, that I cannot treſpaſs upon their patience more than MARKHAM, BLOME, and the other proſe writers upon this ſubject.

IT is moſt certain, that hunting was the exerciſe of the greateſt heroes in antiquity. By this they formed themſelves for war; and their exploits againſt wild beaſts were a prelude to their other victories. XENOPHON ſays, that almoſt all the ancient heroes, NESTOR, THESEUS, CASTOR, POLLUX, ULYSSES, DIOMEDES, ACHILLES, &c. were Μαθηλαὶ Κυνηγεσιῶν, diſciples of hunting; being taught carefully that art, as what would be highly ſerviceable to them in military diſcipline. XEN. CYNEGETIC. And PLINY obſerves, thoſe who were deſigned for great captains, were firſt taught *certare cum fugacibus feris curſu, cum audacibus robore, cum callidis aſtu:* to conteſt with the ſwifteſt wild beaſts, in ſpeed; with the boldeſt, in ſtrength; with the moſt cunning, in craft and ſubtilty. PLIN. PANEGYR. And the ROMAN emperors, in those monuments they erected to transmit their actions to future ages, made no scruple to join the glories of the chace to their most celebrated triumphs. Neither were their poets wanting to do justice to this heroick exercise. Beside that of OPPIAN in GREEK, we have several poems in LATIN upon hunting. GRATIUS was contemporary with OVID; as appears by this verse,

Aptaque venanti GRATIUS *arma dabit.*
LIB. IV. PONT.

GRATIUS shall arm the huntsman for the chace.

But of his works only some fragments remain. There are many others of more modern Date. Amongst these NEMESIANUS, who seems very much superior to GRATIUS, though of a more degenerate age. But only a fragment of his first book is preserved. We might indeed have expected to have seen it treated more at large by VIRGIL in his third Georgick, since it is expresly part of his subject. But he has favoured us only with ten verses; and what he says of dogs, relates wholly to greyhounds and mastiffs.

Veloces

Veloces Spartæ catulos, acremque Molossum.
GEORG. III.

The greyhound ſwift, and maſtiff's furious breed.

And he directs us to feed them with butter-milk. *Paſce ſero pingui.* He has, it is true, touched upon the Chace in the 4th and 7th books of the Æneid. But it is evident, that the art of hunting is very different now from what it was in his days, and very much altered and improved in theſe latter ages. It does not appear to me that the ancients had any notion of purſuing wild beaſts by the ſcent only, with a regular and well-diſciplined pack of hounds; and therefore they muſt have paſſed for poachers amongſt our modern ſportſmen. The muſter-roll given us by OVID, in his ſtory of ACTÆON, is of all ſorts of dogs, and of all countries. And the deſcription of the ancient hunting, as we find it in the antiquities of Pere de MONTFAUCON taken from the Sepulchre of the NASOS, and the Arch of CONSTANTINE, has not the leaſt trace of the manner now in uſe.

WHENEVER the ancients mention dogs followed by the ſcent, they mean no more than finding out the game by the noſe of one ſingle dog. This was as much as they knew of the *odora canum vis*. Thus NEMESIANUS ſays,

Odorato noſcunt veſtigia prato,
Atque etiam leporum ſecreta cubilia monſtrant.

They challenge on the mead the recent ſtains,
And trail the hare unto her ſecret form.

OPPIAN has a long deſcription of theſe dogs in his firſt book, from *ver.* 479 to 526. And here, though he ſeems to deſcribe the hunting of the hare by the ſcent through many turnings and windings; yet he really ſays no more, than that one of thoſe hounds, which he calls ἰχνευτῆρες, finds out the game. For he follows the ſcent no further than the hare's form; from whence, after he has ſtarted her, he purſues her by ſight. I am indebted for theſe two laſt remarks to a reverend and very learned gentleman, whoſe judgment in the *belles lettres* nobody diſputes, and whoſe approbation gave me the aſſurance to publiſh this poem.

OPPIAN alſo obſerves, that the beſt ſort of theſe finders were brought from BRITAIN; this

this iſland having always been famous (as it is at this day) for the beſt breed of hounds, for perſons the beſt ſkilled in the art of hunting, and for horſes the moſt enduring to follow the chace. It is therefore ſtrange that none of our poets have yet thought it worth their while to treat of this ſubject; which is without doubt very noble in itſelf, and very well adapted to receive the moſt beautiful turns of poetry. Perhaps our poets have no great genius for hunting. Yet I hope, my brethren of the couples, by encouraging this firſt, but imperfect, eſſay, will ſhew the world they have at leaſt ſome taſte for poetry.

THE ancients eſteemed hunting, not only as a manly and warlike exerciſe, but as highly conducive to health. The famous GALEN recommends it above all others as not only exerciſing the body, but giving delight and entertainment to the mind. And he calls the inventors of this art wiſe men, and well-ſkilled in human nature. *Lib. de parvæ pilæ exercitio.*

THE gentlemen, who are fond of a gingle at the cloſe of every verſe, and think no poem truly

truly musical but what is in rhyme, will here find themselves disappointed. If they be pleased to read over the short preface before the PARADISE LOST, Mr. SMITH's poem in memory of his friend Mr. JOHN PHILIPS, and the Archbishop of CAMBRAY's letter to Monsieur FONTENELLE, they may probably be of another opinion. For my own part, I shall not be ashamed to follow the example of MILTON, PHILIPS, THOMSON, and all our best tragick writers.

SOME few terms of art are dispersed here and there; but such only as are absolutely requisite to explain my subject. I hope in this the criticks will excuse me; for I am humbly of opinion, that the affectation, and not the necessary use, is the proper object of their censure.

BUT I have done. I know the impatience of my brethren, when a fine day, and the concert of the kennel, invite them abroad. I shall therefore leave my reader to such diversion as he may find in the poem itself.

En age, segnes,
Rumpe moras; vocat ingenti clamore Cithæron,

 Taygetique

Taygetique canes, domitrixque Epidaurus equorum;
Et vox assensu nemorum ingeminata remugit.
VIRG. Georg. III.

Hark, away,
Cast far behind the lingering cares of life.
CITHÆRON calls aloud, and in full cry
Thy hounds, TAYGETUS. EPIDAURUS trains
For us the gen'rous steed; the hunter's shouts,
And chearing cries, assenting woods return.

TO

WILLIAM SOMERVILE, Esq;

ON HIS POEM CALLED

THE CHACE.

WHILE you, Sir, gain the steep ascent to fame,
And honours due to deathless merit claim;
To a weak Muse a kind indulgence lend,
Fond with just praise your labours to commend,
And tell the world, that SOMERVILE's her friend.
Her incense guiltless of the forms of art
Breathes all the huntsman's honesty of heart;
Whose fancy still the pleasing scene retains
Of EDRIC's villa and ARDENNA's plains:
Joys, which from change superior charms receiv'd,
The horn hoarse sounding by the lyre reliev'd:
When the day crown'd with rural chaste delight,
Resigns obsequious to the festive night;
The festive night awakes th' harmonious lay,
And in sweet verse recounts the triumphs of the day.

STRANGE!

STRANGE! that the BRITISH Muſe ſhould
leave ſo long,
The Chace, the ſport of BRITAIN's kings, unſung!
Diſtinguiſh'd land! by Heav'n indulg'd to breed
The ſtout, ſagacious hound, and gen'rous ſteed;
In vain! while yet no bard adorn'd our iſle,
To celebrate the glorious ſylvan toil.
For this what darling ſon ſhall feel thy fire,
God of th' unerring bow, and tuneful lyre?
Our vows are heard—Attend, ye vocal throng,
SOMERVILE meditates th' advent'rous ſong.
Bold to attempt, and happy to excell,
His num'rous verſe the huntſman's art ſhall tell.
From him, ye BRITISH youths, a vig'rous race,
Imbibe the various ſcience of the chace;
And while the well-plann'd ſyſtem you admire,
Know BRUNSWICK only could the work inſpire:
A Georgick Muſe awaits AUGUSTAN days,
And SOMERVILES will ſing, when FREDERICKS
give the bays.

JOHN NIXON.

TO THE AUTHOR OF THE CHACE.

ONCE more, my friend, I touch the trembling lyre,
And in my boſom feel poetic fire.
For thee I quit the law's more rugged ways,
To pay my humble tribute to thy lays.
What, tho' I daily turn each learned ſage,
And labour through the unenlighten'd page:
Wak'd by thy lines, the borrow'd flames I feel,
As flints give fire when aided by the ſteel.
Tho' in ſulphureous clouds of ſmoke confin'd,
Thy rural ſcenes ſpring freſh into my mind.
Thy genius in ſuch colours paints the chace,
The real to fictitious joys give place.
When the wild muſick charms my raviſh'd ear,
How dull, how taſteleſs HANDEL's notes appear!
Ev'n FARENELLI's ſelf the palm reſigns,
He yields—but to the muſick of thy lines.

If

If friends to poetry can yet be found ;
Who without blushing sense prefer to sound ;
Then let this soft, this soul-enfeebling band,
These warbling minstrels quit the beggar'd land.
They but a momentary joy impart,
'Tis you, who touch the soul, and warm the heart.
How tempting do thy sylvan sports appear !
Ev'n wild Ambition might vouchsafe an ear,
Might her fond lust of pow'r a while compose,
And gladly change it for thy sweet repose.
No fierce, unruly senates, threaten here,
No axe, no scaffold, to the view appear,
No envy, disappointment and despair.
Here, blest vicissitude, whene'er you please,
You step from exercise to learned ease :
Turn o'er each classic page, each beauty trace,
The mind unwearied in the pleasing chace.
Oh ! would kind Heav'n such happiness bestow,
Let fools, let knaves, be masters here below.
Grandeur and place, those baits to catch the wise,
And all their pageant train, I pity and despise.

J. TRACY.

The Argument of the First Book.

THE subject proposed. Address to his Royal Highness the Prince. The origin of hunting. The rude and unpolished manner of the first hunters. Beasts at first hunted for food and sacrifice. The grant made by God to man of the beasts, &c. *The regular manner of hunting first brought into this island by the* NORMANS. *The best hounds and best horses bred here. The advantage of this exercise to us, as islanders. Address to gentlemen of estates. Situation of the kennel and its several courts. The diversion and employment of hounds in the kennel. The different sorts of hounds for each different chace. Description of a perfect hound. Of sizing and sorting of hounds, the middle-sized hound recommended. Of the large deep-mouth'd hound for hunting the stag and otter. Of the lime-hound; their use on the borders of* ENGLAND *and* SCOTLAND. *A physical account of scents. Of good and bad scenting days. A short admonition to my brethren of the couples.*

THE CHACE.

A POEM.

THE CHACE I ſing, Hounds, and their various breed,
And no leſs various uſe. O thou Great Prince!
Whom CAMBRIA's tow'ring hills proclaim their lord,
Deign thou to hear my bold, inſtructive ſong.
While grateful citizens with pompous ſhew,
Rear the triumphal arch, rich with th' exploits
Of thy illuſtrious houſe; while virgins pave
Thy way with flow'rs, and, as the Royal Youth
Paſſing they view, admire, and ſigh in vain;
While crowded theatres, too fondly proud
Of their exotick minſtrels, and ſhrill pipes,

The price of manhood, hail thee with a ſong,
And airs ſoft-warbling; my hoarſe-ſounding horn
Invites thee to the Chace, the ſport of kings;
Image of war, without its guilt. The Muſe
Aloft on wing ſhall ſoar, conduct with care
Thy foaming courſer o'er the ſteepy rock,
Or on the river bank receive thee ſafe,
Light-bounding o'er the wave, from ſhore to ſhore.
Be thou our great protector, gracious Youth!
And if in future times, ſome envious prince,
Careleſs of right and guileful, ſhou'd invade
Thy BRITAIN's commerce, or ſhou'd ſtrive in vain
To wreſt the balance from thy equal hand;
Thy hunter-train, in chearful green array'd,
(A band undaunted, and inur'd to toils)
Shall compaſs thee around, die at thy feet,
Or hew thy paſſage thro' th' embattled foe,
And clear thy way to fame; inſpir'd by thee
The nobler chace of glory ſhall purſue
Thro' fire, and ſmoke, and blood, and fields of death.

NATURE,

Nature, in her productions ſlow, aſpires
By juſt degrees to reach Perfection's height:
So mimick Art works leiſurely, till Time
Improve the piece, or wiſe Experience give
The proper finiſhing. When Nimrod bold,
That mighty hunter, firſt made war on beaſts,
And ſtain'd the wood-land green with purple dye,
New, and unpoliſh'd was the huntſman's art;
No ſtated rule, his wanton will his guide.
With clubs and ſtones, rude implements of war,
He arm'd his ſavage bands, a multitude
Untrain'd; of twining oſiers form'd, they pitch
Their artleſs toils, then range the deſert hills,
And ſcow'r the plains below; the trembling herd
Start at th' unuſual ſound, and clam'rous ſhout
Unheard before; ſurpriz'd alas! to find
Man now their foe, whom erſt they deem'd their lord,
But mild and gentle, and by whom as yet
Secure they graz'd. Death ſtretches o'er the plain

Wide-waſting, and grim ſlaughter red with blood:
Urg'd on by hunger keen, they wound, they kill,
Their rage licentious knows no bound; at laſt
Incumber'd with their ſpoils, joyful they bear
Upon their ſhoulders broad, the bleeding prey.
Part on their altars ſmokes a ſacrifice
To that all-gracious Pow'r, whoſe bounteous hand
Supports his wide creation; what remains
On living coals they broil, inelegant
Of taſte, nor ſkill'd as yet in nicer arts
Of pamper'd luxury. Devotion pure,
And ſtrong neceſſity, thus firſt began
The chace of beaſts: tho' bloody was the deed,
Yet without guilt. For the green herb alone
Unequal to ſuſtain man's lab'ring race,
*Now ev'ry moving thing that liv'd on earth
Was granted him for food. So juſt is Heav'n,
To give us in proportion to our wants.

* Gen. chap. ix. ver. 3.

Or

Or chance or induſtry in after-times
Some few improvements made, but ſhort as yet
Of due perfection. In this iſle remote
Our painted anceſtors were ſlow to learn,
To arms devote, of the politer arts
Nor ſkill'd nor ſtudious; till from Neustria's coaſts
Victorious William, to more decent rules
Subdu'd our Saxon fathers, taught to ſpeak
The proper dialect, with horn and voice
To chear the buſy hound, whoſe well-known cry
His liſt'ning peers approve with joint acclaim.
From him ſucceſſive huntſmen learn'd to join
In bloody ſocial leagues, the multitude
Diſpers'd, to ſize, to ſort their various tribes,
To rear, feed, hunt, and diſcipline the pack.

Hail, happy Britain! highly favour'd iſle,
And Heav'n's peculiar care! To thee 'tis giv'n

To train the ſprightly ſteed, more fleet than thoſe
Begot by winds, or the celeſtial breed
That bore the great Pelides thro' the preſs
Of heroes arm'd, and broke their crowded ranks;
Which proudly neighing, with the ſun begins
Chearful his courſe; and ere his beams decline,
Has meaſur'd half thy ſurface unfatigued.
In thee alone, fair land of liberty!
Is bred the perfect hound, in ſcent and ſpeed
As yet unrivall'd, while in other climes
Their virtue fails, a weak degen'rate race.
In vain malignant ſteams, and winter fogs
Load the dull air, and hover round our coaſts,
The huntſman ever gay, robuſt, and bold,
Defies the noxious vapour, and confides
In this delightful exerciſe, to raiſe
His drooping herd and chear his heart with joy.

Ye vig'rous youths, by ſmiling Fortune bleſt
With large demeſnes, hereditary wealth,

Heap'd

Heap'd copious by your wiſe fore-fathers care,
Hear and attend! while I the means reveal
T'enjoy thoſe pleaſures, for the weak too ſtrong,
Too coſtly for the poor: To rein the ſteed
Swift-ſtretching o'er the plain, to chear the pack
Op'ning in conſorts of harmonious joy,
But breathing death. What tho' the gripe ſevere
Of brazen-fiſted Time, and ſlow diſeaſe
Creeping thro' ev'ry vein, and nerve unſtrung,
Afflict my ſhatter'd frame, undaunted ſtill,
Fix'd as a mountain aſh, that braves the bolts
Of angry Jove; tho' blaſted, yet unfallen;
Still can my ſoul in Fancy's mirrour view
Deeds glorious once, recal the joyous ſcene
In all its ſplendors deck'd, o'er the full bowl
Recount my triumphs paſt, urge others on
With hand and voice, and point the winding way:
Pleas'd with that ſocial ſweet garrulity,
The poor diſbanded vet'ran's ſole delight.

First let the Kennel be the huntſman's care,
Upon ſome little eminence erect,
And fronting to the ruddy dawn; its courts
On either hand wide op'ning to receive
The ſun's all-chearing beams, when mild he ſhines,
And gilds the mountain tops. For much the pack
(Rous'd from their dark alcoves) delight to ſtretch,
And baſk, in his invigorating ray:
Warn'd by the ſtreaming light, and merry lark,
Forth ruſh the jolly clan; with tuneful throats
They carol loud, and in grand chorus join'd
Salute the new-born day. For not alone
The vegetable world, but men and brutes
Own his reviving influcnce, and joy
At his approach. Fountain of light! if chance
Some envious cloud veil they refulgent brow,
In vain the muſes aid, untouch'd, unſtrung,
Lies my mute harp, and thy deſponding bard
Sits darkly muſing o'er th' unfiniſh'd lay.

Let

Book 1st page 9.

A. Walker del. et Sculp.

Let no Corinthian pillars prop the dome,
A vain expence, on charitable deeds
Better diſpos'd, to clothe the tatter'd wretch,
Who ſhrinks beneath the blaſt, to feed the poor
Pinch'd with afflictive want: For uſe, not ſtate,
Gracefully plain, let each apartment riſe,
O'er all let cleanlineſs preſide, no ſcraps
Beſtrew the pavement, and no half-pick'd bones,
To kindle fierce debate, or to diſguſt
That nicer ſenſe, on which the ſportſman's hope,
And all his future triumphs muſt depend.
Soon as the growling pack with eager joy
Have lapp'd their ſmoking viands, morn or eve,
From the full ciſtern lead the ductile ſtreams,
To waſh thy court well pav'd, nor ſpare thy pains,
For much to health will cleanlineſs avail.
Seek'ſt thou for hounds to climb the rocky ſteep,
And bruſh th' entangled covert, whoſe nice ſcent
O'er greaſy fallows, and frequented roads

Can pick the dubious way? Banifh far off
Each noifome ftench, let no offenfive fmell
Invade thy wide inclofure, but admit
The nitrous air, and purifying breeze.

Water and fhade no lefs demand thy care:
In a large fquare th' adjacent field inclofe,
There plant in equal ranks the fpreading elm,
Or fragrant lime; moft happy thy defign,
If at the bottom of thy fpacious court,
A large canal fed by the cryftal brook,
From its tranfparent bofom fhall reflect
Downward thy ftructure and inverted grove.
Here when the fun's too potent gleams annoy
The crowded kennel, and the drooping pack,
Reftlefs and faint, loll their unmoiften'd tongues,
And drop their feeble tails, to cooler fhades
Lead forth the panting tribe; foon fhalt thou find
The cordial breeze their fainting hearts revive:

Tu-

Tumultuous ſoon they plunge into the ſtream,
There lave their reeking ſides, with greedy joy
Gulp down the flying wave, this way and that
From ſhore to ſhore they ſwim, while clamour, cloud
And wild uproar torments the troubled flood:
Then on the ſunny band they roll and ſtretch
Their dripping limbs, or elſe in wanton rings
Courſing around, purſuing and purſu'd,
The merry multitude diſporting play.

But here with watchful and obſervant eye,
Attend their frolicks, which too often end
In bloody broils and death. High o'er thy head
Wave thy reſounding whip, and with a voice
Fierce-menacing o'er-rule the ſtern debate,
And quench their kindling rage; for oft in ſport
Begun, combat enſues, growling they ſnarl,
Then on their haunches rear'd, rampant they ſeize
Each other's throats, with teeth, and claws, in gore

Beſmcar'd,

Beſmear'd, they wound, they tear, till on the ground,
Panting, half dead the conquer'd champion lies:
Then ſudden all the baſe ignoble crowd
Loud-clam'ring ſeize the helpleſs worried wretch,
And thirſting for his blood, drag diff'rent ways
His mangled carcaſs on th' enſanguin'd plain.
O breaſts of pity void! t' oppreſs the weak,
To point your vengeance at the friendleſs head,
And with one mutual cry inſult the fall'n!
Emblem too juſt of man's degen'rate race.

Others apart by native inſtinct led,
Knowing inſtructor! 'mong the ranker graſs
Cull each ſalubrious plant, with bitter juice
Concoctive ſtor'd, and potent to allay
Each vicious ferment. Thus the hand divine
Of Providence, beneficent and kind
To all his creatures, for the brutes preſcribes

A ready remedy, and is himſelf
Their great phyſician. Now grown ſtiff with age,
And many a painful chace, the wiſe old hound,
Regardleſs of the frolick pack, attends
His maſter's ſide, or ſlumbers at his eaſe
Beneath the bending ſhade; there many a ring
Runs o'er in dreams; now on the doubtful ſoil
Puzzles perplex'd, or doubles intricate
Cautious unfolds, then wing'd with all his ſpeed,
Bounds o'er the lawn to ſeize his panting prey:
And in imperfect whimp'rings ſpeaks his joy.

A diff'rent hound for ev'ry diff'rent chace
Select with judgment; nor the tim'rous hare
O'ermatch'd deſtroy, but leave that vile offence
To the mean, murd'rous, courſing crew; intent
On blood and ſpoil. O blaſt their hopes, juſt Heav'n!
And all their painful drudgeries repay

With disappointment and severe remorse.
But husband thou thy pleasures, and give scope
To all her subtle play: by nature led
A thousand shifts she tries; t' unravel these
Th' industrious beagle twists his waving tail.
Thro' all her labyrinths pursues, and rings
Her doleful knell. See there with count'nance blithe,
And with a courtly grin, the fawning hound
Salutes thee cow'ring, his wide op'ning nose
Upward he curls, and his large sloe-black eyes
Melt in soft blandishments, and humble joy;
His glossy skin, or yellow-pied, or blue,
In lights or shades by Nature's pencil drawn,
Reflects the various tints; his ears and legs
Fleckt here and there, in gay enamel'd pride,
Rival the speckled pard; his rush-grown tail
O'er his broad back bends in an ample arch;
On shoulders clean, upright and firm he stands;

His

His round cat' foot, ſtrait hams, and wide-ſpread
thighs,
And his low-dropping cheſt, confeſs his ſpeed,
His ſtrength, his wind, or on the ſteepy hill,
Or far-extended plain; in ev'ry part
So well proportion'd, that the nicer ſkill
Of Phidias himſelf can't blame thy choice.
Of ſuch compoſe thy pack. But here a mean
Obſerve, nor the large hound prefer, of ſize
Gigantick; he in the thick-woven covert
Painfully tugs, or in the thorny brake
Torn and embarraſs'd bleeds: But if too ſmall,
The pigmy brood in ev'ry furrow ſwims;
Moil'd in the clogging clay, panting they lag
Behind inglorious; or elſe ſhivering creep
Benumb'd and faint beneath the ſhelt'ring thorn.
For hounds of middle ſize, active and ſtrong,
Will better anſwer all thy various ends,
And crown thy pleaſing labours with ſucceſs.

As ſome brave captain, curious and exact,
By his fix'd ſtandard forms in equal ranks
His gay battalion, as one man they move
Step after ſtep, their ſize the ſame, their arms
Far-gleaming, dart the ſame united blaze:
Reviewing generals his merit own;
How regular! how juſt! And all his cares
Are well repaid, if mighty George approve.
So model thou thy pack, if honour touch
Thy gen'rous ſoul, and the world's juſt applauſe.
But above all take heed, nor mix thy hounds
Of diff'rent kinds; diſcordant ſounds ſhall grate
Thy ears offended, and a lagging line
Of babbling curs diſgrace thy broken pack.
But if th' amphibious otter be thy chace,
Or ſtately ſtag, that o'er the woodland reigns;
Or if the harmonious thunder of the field
Delight thy raviſh'd ears; the deep-flew'd hound
Breed up with care, ſtrong, heavy, ſlow, but ſure;

Whoſe ears down-hanging from his thick round head
Shall ſweep the morning dew, whoſe clanging voice
Awake the mountain echo in her cell,
And ſhake the foreſts: The bold Talbot kind
Of theſe the prime, as white as ALPINE ſnows;
And great their uſe of old. Upon the banks
Of TWEED, ſlow winding thro' the vale, the ſeat
Of war and rapine once, ere BRITONS knew
The ſweets of peace, or ANNA's dread commands
To laſting leagues the haughty rivals aw'd,
There dwelt a pilf'ring race; well-train'd and ſkill'd
In all the myſteries of theft, the ſpoil
Their only ſubſtance, feuds and war their ſport:
Not more expert in ev'ry fraudful art

Th' arch * felon was of old, who by the tail
Drew back his lowing prize: In vain his wiles,
In vain the ſhelter of the cov'ring rock,
In vain the ſooty cloud, and ruddy flames
That iſſu'd from his mouth; for ſoon he paid
His forfeit life: A debt how juſtly due
To wrong'd Alcides, and avenging Heav'n!
Veil'd in the ſhades of night they ford the ſtream,
Then prowling far and near, whate'er they ſeize
Becomes their prey; nor flocks nor herds are
ſafe,
Nor ſtalls protect the ſteer, nor ſtrong barr'd doors
Secure the fav'rite horſe. Soon as the morn
Reveals his wrongs, with ghaſtly viſage wan
The plunder'd owner ſtands, and from his lips
A thouſand thronging curſes burſt their way:
He calls his ſtout allies, and in a line
His faithful hound he leads, then with a voice

* Cacus, Virg. Æn. Lib. VIII.

That

That utters loud his rage, attentive chears:
Soon the ſagacious brute, his curling tail
Flouriſh'd in air, low-bending plies around
His buſy noſe, the ſteaming vapour ſnuffs
Inquiſitive, nor leaves one turf untried,
Till conſcious of the recent ſtains, his heart
Beats quick; his ſnuffling noſe, his active tail
Atteſt his joy; then with deep op'ning mouth,
That makes the welkin tremble, he proclaims
Th' audacious felon; foot by foot he marks
His winding way, while all the liſt'ning crowd
Applaud his reaſ'nings. O'er the wat'ry ford,
Dry ſandy heaths, and ſtony barren hills,
O'er beaten paths, with men and beaſts diſtain'd,
Unerring he purſues; till at the cot
Arriv'd, and ſeizing by his guilty throat
The caitif vile, redeems the captive prey:
So exquiſitely delicate his ſenſe!

Shou'd ſome more curious ſportſman here enquire,
Whence this ſagacity, this wond'rous pow'r
Of tracing ſtep by ſtep, or man or brute?
What guide inviſible points out their way,
O'er the dank marſh, bleak hill, and ſandy plain?
The courteous Muſe ſhall the dark cauſe reveal.
The blood that from the heart inceſſant rolls
In many a crimſon tide, then here and there
In ſmaller rills diſparted, as it flows
Propell'd, the ſerous particles evade
Thro' th' open pores, and with the ambient air
Entangling mix. As fuming vapours riſe,
And hang upon the gently purling brook,
There by th' incumbent atmoſphere compreſs'd.
The panting chace grows warmer as he flies,
And thro' the net-work of the ſkin perſpires;
Leaves a long-ſtreaming trail behind, which by
The cooler air condens'd, remains, unleſs

By ſome rude ſtorm diſpers'd, or rarified
By the meridian ſun's intenſer heat.
To ev'ry ſhrub the warm effluvia cling,
Hang on the graſs, impregnate earth and ſkies.
With noſtrils op'ning wide, o'er hill, o'er dale
The vig'rous hounds purſue, with ev'ry breath
Inhale the grateful ſteam, quick pleaſures ſting
Their tingling nerves, while they their thanks repay,
And in triumphant melody confeſs
The titillating joy. Thus on the air
Depend the hunter's hopes. When ruddy ſtreaks
At eve forebode a bluſt'ring ſtormy day,
Or low'ring clouds blacken the mountain's brow,
When nipping froſts, and the keen biting blaſts
Of the dry parching eaſt, menace the trees
With tender bloſſoms teeming, kindly ſpare
Thy ſleeping pack, in their warm beds of ſtraw
Low-ſinking at their eaſe; liſtleſs they ſhrink

Into ſome dark receſs, nor hear thy voice
Tho' oft invok'd; or haply if thy call
Rouſe up the ſlumb'ring tribe, with heavy eyes
Glaz'd, lifeleſs, dull, downward they drop their
tails
Inverted; high on their bent backs erect
Their pointed briſtles ſtare, or 'mong the tufts
Of ranker weeds, each ſtomach-healing plant
Curious they crop, ſick, ſpiritleſs, forlorn.
Theſe inauſpicious days, on other cares
Employ thy precious hours; th' improving friend
With open arms embrace, and from his lips
Glean ſcience, ſeaſon'd with good-natur'd wit.
But if th' inclement ſkies and angry JOVE
Forbid the pleaſing intercourſe, thy books
Invite thy ready hand, each ſacred page
Rich with the wiſe remarks of heroes old.
Converſe familiar with th' illuſtrious dead;
With great examples of old GREECE or ROME

Enlarge

Enlarge thy free-born heart, and bleſs kind Heav'n,
That Britain yet enjoys dear Liberty,
That balm of life, that ſweeteſt bleſſing, cheap
Tho' purchas'd with our blood. Well-bred, polite,
Credit thy calling. See! how mean, how low,
The bookleſs ſaunt'ring youth, proud of the ſkut
That dignifies his cap, his flouriſh'd belt,
And ruſty couples gingling by his ſide.
Be thou of other mold; and know that ſuch
Tranſporting pleaſures were by Heav'n ordain'd
Wiſdom's relief, and Virtue's great reward.

The ARGUMENT of the Second Book.

OF the power of instinct in brutes. Two remarkable instances in the hunting of the roebuck, and in the hare going to seat in the morning. Of the variety of seats or forms of the hare, according to the change of the season, weather, or wind. Description of the hare-hunting in all its parts, interspersed with rules to be observed by those who follow that chace. Transition to the ASIATICK *way of hunting, particularly the magnificent manner of the Great Mogul, and other* TARTARIAN *princes, taken from Monsieur* BERNIER, *and the history of* GENGISKAN *the Great. Concludes with a short reproof of tyrants and oppressors of mankind.*

BOOK

BOOK THE SECOND.

NOR will it leſs delight th' attentive ſage
T' obſerve that Inſtinct, which unerring guides
The brutal race, which mimicks reaſon's lore
And oft tranſcends: Heav'n-taught the roe-buck ſwift
Loiters at eaſe before the driving pack
And mocks their vain purſuit, nor far he flies
But checks his ardour, till the ſteaming ſcent
That freſhens on the blade, provokes their rage.
Urg'd to their ſpeed, his weak deluded foes
Soon flag fatigued; ſtrain'd to exceſs each nerve,
Each ſlacken'd ſinew fails; they pant, they foam;
Then o'er the lawn he bounds, o'er the high hills

Stretches ſecure, and leaves the ſcatter'd crowd
To puzzle in the diſtant vale below.

'Tis Inſtinct that directs the jealous hare
To chuſe her ſoft abode: With ſtep revers'd
She forms the doubling maze; then, ere the morn
Peeps thro' the clouds, leaps to her cloſe receſs.

As wand'ring ſhepherds on th' Arabian plains
No ſettled reſidence obſerve, but ſhift
Their moving camp, now, on ſome cooler hill
With cedars crown'd, court the refreſhing breeze;
And then, below, where trickling ſtreams diſtil
From ſome penurious ſource, their thirſt allay,
And feed their fainting flocks: So the wiſe hares
Oft quit their ſeats, leſt ſome more curious eye
Shou'd mark their haunts, and by dark treach'rous wiles
Plot their deſtruction; or perchance in hopes

Of plenteous forage, near the ranker mead,
Or matted blade, wary, and cloſe they ſit.
When ſpring ſhines forth, ſeaſon of love and joy,
In the moiſt marſh, 'mong beds of ruſhes hid,
They cool their boiling blood: When ſummer ſuns
Bake the cleft earth, to thick wide-waving fields
Of corn full-grown, they lead their helpleſs young:
But when autumnal torrents, and fierce rains
Deluge the vale, in the dry crumbling bank
Their forms they delve, and cautiouſly avoid
The dripping covert: Yet when winter's cold
Their limbs benumbs, thither with ſpeed return'd
In the long graſs they ſkulk, or ſhrinking creep
Among the wither'd leaves, thus changing ſtill,
As fancy prompts them, or as food invites.
But ev'ry ſeaſon carefully obſerv'd,
Th' inconſtant winds, the fickle element,
The wiſe experienc'd huntſman ſoon may find
His ſubtle, various game, nor waſte in vain

His tedious hours, till his impatient hounds,
With diſappointment vex'd, each ſpringing lark
Babbling purſue, far ſcatter'd o'er the fields.

Now golden Autumn from her open lap
Her fragrant bounties ſhow'rs; the fields are ſhorn;
Inwardly ſmiling, the proud farmer views
The riſing pyramids that grace his yard,
And counts his large increaſe; his barns are ſtor'd
And groaning ſtaddles bend beneath their load.
All now is free as air, and the gay pack
In the rough briſtly ſtubbles range unblam'd;
No widow's tears o'erflow, no ſecret curſe
Swells in the farmer's breaſt, which his pale lips
Trembling conceal, by his fierce landlord aw'd:
But courteous now he levels ev'ry fence,
Joins in the common cry, and halloos loud,
Charm'd with the rattling thunder of the field.
Oh bear me, ſome kind power inviſible!

To that extended lawn, where the gay court
View the ſwift racers, ſtretching to the goal;
Games more renown'd and a far nobler train,
Than proud ELEAN fields could boaſt of old.
Oh! were a THEBAN lyre not wanting here,
And PINDAR's voice, to do their merit right!
Or to thoſe ſpacious plains, where the ſtrain'd eye
In the wide proſpect loſt, beholds at laſt
SARUM's proud ſpire, that o'er the hills aſcends,
And pierces thro' the clouds. Or to thy downs,
Fair COTSWOLD, where the well-breath'd beagle climbs,
With matchleſs ſpeed, thy green aſpiring brow,
And leaves the lagging multitude behind.

HAIL, gentle Dawn! mild bluſhing goddeſs, hail!
Rejoic'd I ſee thy purple mantle ſpread
O'er half the ſkies, gems pave thy radiant way,

And orient pearls from ev'ry ſhrub depend.
Farewel, Cleora; here deep ſunk in down
Slumber ſecure, with happy dreams amus'd,
Till grateful ſteams ſhall tempt thee to receive
Thy early meal, or thy officious maids,
The toilet plac'd, ſhall urge thee to perform
Th' important work. Me other joys invite,
The horn ſonorous calls, the pack awak'd
Their mattins chant, nor brook my long delay.
My courſer hears their voice; ſee there with ears
And tail erect, neighing he paws the ground;
Fierce rapture kindles in his red'ning eyes,
And boils in ev'ry vein. As captive boys
Cow'd by the ruling rod, and haughty frowns
Of pedagogues ſevere, from their hard taſks
If once diſmiſs'd, no limits can contain
The tumult rais'd within their little breaſts,
But give a looſe to all their frolick play:
So from their kennel ruſh the joyous pack;

A thou-

A thousand wanton gayeties express
Their inward extasy, their pleasing sport
Once more indulg'd, and liberty restor'd.
The rising sun, that o'er th' horizon peeps,
As many colours from their glossy skins
Beaming reflects, as paint the various bow
When April show'rs descend. Delightful scene!
Where all around is gay, men, horses, dogs,
And in each smiling countenance appears
Fresh blooming health, and universal joy.

Huntsman, lead on! behind the clust'ring pack
Submiss attend, hear with respect thy whip
Loud-clanging, and thy harsher voice obey:
Spare not the straggling cur, that wildly roves;
But let thy brisk assistant on his back
Imprint thy just resentments; let each lash
Bite to the quick, till howling he return
And whining creep amid the trembling crowd.

Here on this verdant ſpot, where Nature kind
With double bleſſings crown the farmer's hopes;
Where flow'rs autumnal ſpring, and the rank mead
Affords the wand'ring hares a rich repaſt;
Throw off thy ready pack. See, where they ſpread,
And range around, and daſh the glitt'ring dew.
If ſome ſtanch hound, with his authentick voice,
Avow the recent trail, the juſtling tribe
Attend his call, then with one mutual cry,
The welcome news confirm, and echoing hills
Repeat the pleaſing tale. See how they thread
The brakes, and up yon furrow drive along!
But quick they back recoil, and wiſely check
Their eager haſte; then o'er the fallow'd ground
How leiſurely they work, and many a pauſe
Th' harmonious concert breaks; till more aſſur'd
With joy redoubled the low vallies ring.
What artful labyrinths perplex their way!

Ah!

Ah! there ſhe lies; how cloſe! ſhe pants, ſhe doubts
If now ſhe lives; ſhe trembles as ſhe ſits,
With horror ſeiz'd. The wither'd graſs that clings
Around her head, of the ſame ruſſet hue
Almoſt deceiv'd my ſight, had not her eyes
With life full-beaming her vain wiles betray'd.
At diſtance draw thy pack, let all be huſh'd,
No clamour loud, no frantic joy be heard,
Leſt the wild hound run gadding o'er the plain
Untractable, nor hear thy chiding voice.
Now gently put her off; ſee how direct
To her known Muſe ſhe flies! Here, huntſman, bring
(But without hurry) all thy jolly hounds,
And calmly lay them in. How low they ſtoop,
And ſeem to plough the ground! then all at once
With greedy noſtrils ſnuff the fuming ſteam
That glads their flutt'ring hearts. As winds let looſe
From the dark caverns of the bluſt'ring God,

They burſt away, and ſweep the dewy lawn.
Hope gives them wings while ſhe's ſpurr'd on by
fear.
The welkin rings, men, dogs, hills, rocks, and
woods
In the full concert join. Now, my brave youths,
Stripp'd for the chace, give all your ſouls to joy!
See how their courſers, than the mountain roe
More fleet, the verdant carpet ſkim, thick clouds
Snorting they breathe, their ſhining hoofs ſcarce
print
The graſs unbruis'd; with emulation fir'd
They ſtrain to lead the field, top the barr'd gate,
O'er the deep ditch exulting bound, and bruſh
The thorny-twining hedge: The riders bend
O'er their arch'd necks; with ſteady hands, by
turns
Indulge their ſpeed, or moderate their rage.
Where are their ſorrows, diſappointments, wrongs,

Vexations,

Vexations, ſickneſs, cares? All, all are gone,
And with the panting winds lag far behind

Huntsman! her gait obſerve; if in wide rings
She wheel her mazy way, in the ſame round
Perſiſting ſtill, ſhe'll foil the beaten track.
But if ſhe fly, and with the fav'ring wind
Urge her bold courſe; leſs intricate thy taſk:
Puſh on thy pack. Like ſome poor exil'd wretch
The frighted chace leaves her late dear abodes,
O'er plains remote ſhe ſtretches far away,
Ah! never to return! For greedy Death
Hov'ring exults, ſecure to ſeize his prey.

Hark! from yon covert, where thoſe tow'ring
oaks
Above the humble copſe aſpiring riſe,
What glorious triumphs burſt in ev'ry gale
Upon our raviſh'd ears! The hunters ſhout,

The clanging horns ſwell their ſweet-winding
notes,
The pack wide op'ning load the trembling air
With various melody; from tree to tree
The propagated cry redoubling bounds,
And winged zephyrs waft the floating joy
Thro' all the regions near: afflictive birch
No more the ſchool-boy dreads, his priſon broke,
Scamp'ring he flies, nor heeds his maſter's call;
The weary traveller forgets his road,
And climbs th' adjacent hill; the ploughman leaves
Th' unfiniſh'd furrow; nor his bleating flocks
Are now the ſhepherd's joy; men, boys, and girls
Deſert th' unpeopled village; and wild crowds
Spread o'er the plain, by the ſweet frenzy ſeiz'd.
Look, how ſhe pants! and o'er yon op'ning glade
Slips glancing by; while, at the further end,
The puzzling pack unravel wile by wile,
Maze within maze. The covert's utmoſt bound

Slily

A. Walker del. et Sculp.

Slily ſhe ſkirts; behind them cautious creeps,
And in that very track, ſo lately ſtain'd
By all the ſteaming crowd, ſeems to purſue
The foe ſhe flies. Let cavillers deny
That brutes have reaſon; ſure 'tis ſomething more,
'Tis Heav'n directs, and ſtratagems inſpire,
Beyond the ſhort extent of human thought.
But hold — I ſee her from the covert break;
Sad on yon little eminence ſhe ſits;
Intent ſhe liſtens with one ear erect,
Pond'ring, and doubtful what new courſe to take,
And how t'eſcape the fierce bloody-thirſty crew,
That ſtill urge on, and ſtill in vollies loud
Inſult her woes, and mock her ſore diſtreſs.
As now in louder peals, the loaded winds
Bring on the gath'ring ſtorm, her fears prevail;
And o'er the plain, and o'er the mountain's ridge,
Away ſhe flies; nor ſhips with wind and tide,
And all their canvaſs wings, ſcud half ſo faſt.

Once more, ye jovial train, your courage try,
And each clean courſer's ſpeed. We ſcour along,
In pleaſing hurry and confuſion toſt;
Oblivion to be wiſh'd. The patient pack
Hang on the ſcent unweary'd, up they climb,
And ardent we purſue; our lab'ring ſteeds
We preſs, we gore; till once the ſummit gain'd,
Painfully panting, there we breathe a while;
Then like a foaming torrent, pouring down
Precipitant, we ſmoke along the vale.
Happy the man who with unrival'd ſpeed
Can paſs his fellows, and with pleaſure view
The ſtruggling pack; how in the rapid courſe
Alternate they preſide, and joſtling puſh
To guide the dubious ſcent; how giddy youth
Oft babbling errs, by wiſer age reprov'd;
How niggard of his ſtrength, the wiſe old hound
Hangs in the rear, till ſome important point
Rouſe all his diligence, or till the chace

Sinking he finds: then to the head he ſprings
With thirſt of glory fir'd, and wins the prize.
Huntſman, take heed; they ſtop in full career.
Yon crowding flocks, that at a diſtance gaze,
Have haply foil'd the turf. See! that old hound,
How buſily he works, but dares not truſt
His doubtful ſenſe; draw yet a wider ring.
Hark! now again the chorus fills. As bells
Sally'd a while at once their peal renew,
And high in air the tuneful thunder rolls.
See, how they toſs, with animated rage
Recov'ring all they loſt!—That eager haſte
Some doubling wile foreſhews.—Ah! yet once more
They're check'd,—hold back with ſpeed—on either hand
They flouriſh round—ev'n yet perſiſt—'Tis right,
Away they ſpring; the ruſtling ſtubbles bend
Beneath the driving ſtorm. Now the poor chace
Begins to flag, to her laſt ſhifts reduc'd.

From brake to brake ſhe flies, and viſits all
Her well-known haunts, where once ſhe rang'd ſe-
cure,
With love and plenty bleſt. See! there ſhe goes,
She reels along, and by her gait betrays
Her inward weakneſs. See, how black ſhe looks!
The ſweat that clogs th' obſtructed pores, ſcarce
leaves
A languid ſcent. And now in open view
See, ſee, ſhe flies! each eager hound exerts
His utmoſt ſpeed, and ſtretches ev'ry nerve.
How quick ſhe turns! their gaping jaws eludes,
And yet a moment lives; till round inclos'd
By all the greedy pack, with infant ſcreams
She yields her breath, and there reluctant dies.
So when the furious BACCHANALS aſſail'd
THREICIAN ORPHEUS, poor ill-fated bard!
Loud was the cry, hills, woods, and HEBRUS'
banks,

Return'd their clam'rous rage; diſtreſs'd he flies,
Shifting from place to place, but flies in vain;
For eager they purſue, till panting, faint,
By noiſy multitudes o'erpower'd, he ſinks,
To the relentleſs crowd a bleeding prey.

The huntſman now, a deep inciſion made,
Shakes out with hands impure, and daſhes down
Her reeking entrails, and yet quivering heart.
Theſe claim the pack, the bloody perquiſite
For all their toils. Stretch'd on the ground ſhe lies,
A mangled corſe; in her dim glaring eyes
Cold death exults, and ſtiffens ev'ry limb.
Aw'd by the threat'ning whip, the furious hounds
Around her bay; or at their maſter's foot,
Each happy fav'rite courts his kind applauſe,
With humble adulation cow'ring low.
All now is joy. With cheeks full-blown they wind
Her ſolemn dirge, while the loud-op'ning pack

The concert ſwell, and hills and dales return
The ſadly-pleaſing ſounds. Thus the poor hare,
A puny, daſtard animal, but vers'd
In ſubtle wiles, diverts the youthful train.
But if thy proud, aſpiring ſoul diſdains
So mean a prey, delighted with the pomp,
Magnificence and grandeur of the chace;
Hear what the muſe from faithful records ſings.

WHY on the banks of GEMNA INDIAN ſtream,
Line within line, riſe the pavilions proud,
Their ſilken ſtreamers waving in the wind?
Why neighs the warrior horſe? From tent to tent,
Why preſs in crowds the buzzing multitude?
Why ſhines the poliſh'd helm, and pointed lance,
This way and that far-beaming o'er the plain?
Nor VISAPOUR nor GOLCONDA rebel;
Nor the great SOPHY, with his num'rous hoſt,
Lays waſte the provinces; nor glory fires

To

To rob, and to destroy, beneath the name
And specious guise of war. A nobler cause
Calls AURENGZEBE to arms. No cities sack'd,
No mother's tears, no helpless orphan's cries,
No violated leagues, with sharp remorse
Shall sting the conscious victor: But mankind
Shall hail him good and just. For 'tis on beasts
He draws his vengeful sword; on beasts of prey
Full-fed with human gore. See, see, he comes!
Imperial DEHLI op'ning wide her gates,
Pours out her thronging legions, bright in arms,
And all the pomp of war. Before them sound
Clarions and trumpets, breathing martial airs,
And bold defiance. High upon his throne,
Born on the back of his proud elephant,
Sits the great chief of TAMUR's glorious race:
Sublime he sits, amid the radiant blaze
Of gems and gold. OMRAHS about him crowd,
And rein th' ARABIAN steed, and watch his nod:

And potent Rajahs, who themſelves preſide
O'er realms of wide extent; but here ſubmiſs
Their homage pay, alternate kings and ſlaves.
Next theſe, with prying eunuchs girt around,
The fair ſultanas of his court: a troop
Of choſen beauties, but with care conceal'd
From each intruſive eye; one look is death.
Ah cruel Eastern law (had kings a pow'r
But equal to their wild tyrannick will)
To rob us of the ſun's all-chearing ray,
Were leſs ſevere. The vulgar cloſe the march,
Slaves and artificers; and Dehli mourns
Her empty and depopulated ſtreets.
Now at the camp arriv'd with ſtern review,
Thro' groves of ſpears, from file to file he darts
His ſharp experienc'd eye; their order marks,
Each in his ſtation rang'd, exact and firm,
Till in the boundleſs line his ſight is loſt.
Not greater multitudes in arms appear'd

On

On theſe extended plains, when Ammon's ſon
With mighty Porus in dread battle join'd,
The vaſſal world the prize. Nor was that hoſt
More numerous of old, which the great king*
Pour'd out on Greece from all th' unpeopled East;
That bridg'd the Hellespont from ſhore to ſhore,
And drank the rivers dry. Mean while in troops
The buſy hunter-train mark out the ground,
A wide circumference; full many a league
In compaſs round; woods, rivers, hills and plains.
Large provinces; enough to gratify
Ambition's higheſt aim, could reaſon bound
Man's erring will. Now ſit in cloſe divan
The mighty chiefs of this prodigious hoſt.
He from the throne high-eminent preſides,
Give out his mandates proud, laws of the chace,
From ancient records drawn. With rev'rence low,

* Xerxes.

And

And proſtrate at his feet, the chiefs receive
His irreverſible decrees, from which
To vary, is to die. Then his brave bands
Each to his ſtation leads; encamping round,
Till the wide circle is compleatly form'd.
Where decent order reigns, what theſe command,
Thoſe execute with ſpeed, and punctual care;
In all the ſtricteſt diſcipline of war:
As if ſome watchful foe, with bold inſult,
Hung low'ring o'er their camp. The high reſolve,
That flies on wings thro' all th' encircling line,
Each motion ſteers, and animates the whole.
So by the ſun's attractive pow'r controll'd,
The planets in their ſpheres roll round his orb:
On all he ſhines, and rules the great machine.

Ere yet the morn diſpels the fleeting miſts,
The ſignal giv'n by the loud trumpet's voice,
Now high in air, th' imperial ſtandard waves,

Emblazon'd

Emblazon'd rich with gold, and glittering gems;
And like a ſheet of fire, thro' the dun gloom
Streaming meteorous. The ſoldiers ſhouts,
And all the brazen inſtruments of war,
With mutual clamour, and united din,
Fill the large concave. While from camp to camp,
They catch the varied ſounds, floating in air,
Round all the wide circumference, tygers fell
Shrink at the noiſe, deep in his gloomy den
The lion ſtarts, and morſels yet unchew'd
Drop from his trembling jaws. Now all at once
Onward they march embattled, to the ſound
Of martial harmony; fifes, cornets, drums,
That rouſe the ſleepy ſoul to arms, and bold
Heroick deeds. In parties here and there
Detach'd o'er hill and dale, the hunters range
Inquiſitive; ſtrong dogs that match in fight
The boldeſt brute, around their maſters wait,
A faithful guard. No haunt unſearch'd, they drive

From

From ev'ry covert, and from ev'ry den,
The lurking savages. Incessant shouts
Re-echo thro' the woods, and kindling fire
Gleam from the mountain tops; the forest seems
One mingling blaze: like flocks of sheep they fly
Before the flaming brand: fierce lions, pards,
Boars, tygers, bears, and wolves; a dreadful crew
Of grim blood-thirsty foes; growling along,
They stalk indignant; but fierce vengeance still
Hangs pealing on their rear, and pointed spears
Present immediate death. Soon as the night
Wrapt in her sable veil forbids the chace,
They pitch their tents, in even ranks, around
The circling camp. The guards are plac'd, and fires
At proper distances ascending rise,
And paint the horizon with their ruddy light.
So round some island's shore of large extent,
Amid the gloomy horrors of the night,
The billows breaking on the pointed rocks,

Seem all one flame, and the bright circuit wide
Appears a bulwark of ſurrounding fire.
What dreadful howlings, and what hideous roar,
Diſturb thoſe peaceful ſhades! where erſt the bird
That glads the night, had chear'd the liſt'ning groves
With ſweet complainings. Thro' the ſilent gloom
Oft they the guards aſſail; as oft repell'd
They fly reluctant, with hot-boiling rage
Stung to the quick, and mad with wild deſpair.
Thus day by day, they ſtill the chace renew,
At night encamp; till now in ſtreighter bounds
The circle leſſens, and the beaſts perceive
The wall that hems them in on ev'ry ſide.
And now their fury burſts, and knows no mean;
From man they turn, and point their ill-judg'd rage
Againſt their fellow brutes. With teeth and claws
The civil war begins; grappling they tear.
Lions on tygers prey, and bears on wolves:

Horrible diſcord! till the crowd behind
Shouting purſue, and part the bloody fray.
At once their wrath ſubſides; tame as the lamb
The lion hangs his head, the furious pard,
Cow'd and ſubdu'd, flies from the face of man,
Nor bears one glance of his commanding eye.
So abject is a tyrant in diſtreſs.

At laſt within the narrow plain confin'd,
A liſted field, mark'd out for bloody deeds,
An amphitheatre more glorious far
Than ancient Rome cou'd boaſt, they crowd in heaps,
Diſmay'd, and quite appall'd. In meet array
Sheath'd in refulgent arms, a noble band
Advance; great lords of high imperial blood,
Early reſolv'd t' aſſert their royal race,
And prove by glorious deeds their valour's growth
Mature, ere yet the callow down has ſpread

Its

Its curling shade. On bold ARABIAN steeds
With decent pride they sit, that fearless hear
The lion's dreadful roar; and down the rock
Swift-shooting plunge, or o'er the mountain's ridge
Stretching along, the greedy tyger leave
Panting behind. On foot their faithful slaves
With javelins arm'd attend; each watchful eye
Fix'd on his youthful care, for him alone
He fears, and to redeem his life, unmov'd
Would lose his own. The mighty AURENGZEBE,
From his high-elevated throne, beholds
His blooming race; revolving in his mind
What once he was, in his gay spring of life,
When vigour strung his nerves. Parental joy
Melts in his eyes, and flushes in his cheeks.
Now the loud trumpet sounds a charge. The shouts
Of eager hosts, thro' all the circling line,
And the wild howlings of the beasts within
Rend wide the welkin, flights of arrows, wing'd

With death, and javelins launch'd from ev'ry arm,
Gall ſore the brutal bands, with many a wound
Gor'd thro' and thro'. Deſpair at laſt prevails,
When fainting nature ſhrinks, and rouſes all
Their drooping courage. Swell'd with furious rage,
Their eyes dart fire; and on the youthful band
They ruſh implacable. They their broad ſhields
Quick interpoſe; on each devoted head
Their flaming falchions, as the bolts of Jove,
Deſcend unerring. Proſtrate on the ground
The grinning monſters lie, and their foul gore
Defiles the verdant plain. Nor idle ſtand
The truſty ſlaves; with pointed ſpears they pierce
Thro' their tough hides; or at their gaping mouths
An eaſier paſſage find. The king of brutes
In broken roarings breathes his laſt; the bear
Grumbles in death; nor can his ſpotted ſkin,
Tho' ſleek it ſhine, with varied beauties gay,
Save the proud pard from unrelenting fate.

The battle bleeds, grim Slaughter ſtrides along,
Glutting her greedy jaws, grins o'er her prey.
Men, horſes, dogs, fierce beaſts of ev'ry kind,
A ſtrange promiſcuous carnage, drench'd in blood,
And heaps on heaps amaſs'd. What yet remain
Alive, with vain aſſault contend to break
Th' impenetrable line. Others, whom fear
Inſpires with ſelf-preſerving wiles, beneath
The bodies of the ſlain for ſhelter creep.
Aghaſt they fly, or hide their heads diſpers'd.
And now perchance (had heav'n but pleas'd) the work
Of death had been compleat; and AURENGZEBE
By one dread frown extinguiſh'd half their race.
When lo! the bright ſultanas of his court
Appear, and to his raviſh'd eyes diſplay
Thoſe charms but rarely to the day reveal'd.

Lowly they bend, and humbly sue, to save
The vanquish'd host. What mortal can deny
When suppliant beauty begs? At his command
Op'ning to right and left, the well-train'd troops
Leave a large void for their retreating foes.
Away they fly, on wings of fear upborn,
To seek on distant hills their late abodes.

Ye proud oppressors, whose vain hearts exult
In wantonness of pow'r, 'gainst the brute race,
Fierce robbers like yourselves, a guiltless war
Wage uncontroll'd: here quench your thirst of blood;
But learn from Aurengzebe to spare mankind.

The ARGUMENT of the Third Book.

OF King EDGAR, *and his imposing a tribute of wolves heads upon the kings of* WALES: *from hence a transition to fox-hunting, which is described in all its parts. Censure of an over-numerous pack. Of the several engines to destroy foxes, and other wild beasts. The steel-trap described, and the manner of using it. Description of the pitfall for the lion; and another for the elephant. The ancient way of hunting the tyger with a mirror. The* ARABIAN *manner of hunting the wild boar. Description of the royal stag-chace at* WINDSOR FOREST. *Concludes with an address to his majesty, and an eulogy upon mercy.*

BOOK THE THIRD.

IN ALBION's isle when glorious EDGAR reign'd,
He, wisely provident, from her white cliffs
Launch'd half her forests, and with num'rous fleets
Cover'd his wide domain: there proudly rode
Lord of the deep, the great prerogative
Of BRITISH monarchs. Each invader bold,
DANE and NORWEGIAN, at a distance gaz'd,
And disappointed, gnash'd his teeth in vain.
He scour'd the seas, and to remotest shores
With swelling sails the trembling corsair fled.
Rich commerce flourish'd; and with busy oars
Dash'd the resounding surge. Nor less at land
His royal cares; wise, potent, gracious prince!
His subjects from their cruel foes he sav'd,

And from rapacious ſavages their flocks.
Cambria's proud kings (tho' with reluctance) paid
Their tributary wolves; head after head,
In full account, till the woods yield no more,
And all the rav'nous race extinct is loſt.
In fertile paſtures, more ſecurely graz'd
The ſocial troops; and ſoon their large increaſe
With curling fleeces whiten'd all the plains.
But yet, alas! the wily fox remain'd,
A ſubtle, pilf'ring foe prowling around
In midnight ſhades, and wakeful to deſtroy.
In the full fold, the poor defenceleſs lamb,
Seiz'd by his guileful arts, with ſweet warm blood
Supplies a rich repaſt. The mournful ewe,
Her deareſt treaſure loſt, thro' the dun night
Wanders perplex'd, and darkling bleats in vain:
While in th' adjacent buſh, poor Philomel,
(Herſelf a parent once, till wanton churls

Deſpoil'd her neſt) joins in her loud laments,
With ſweeter notes, and more melodious woe.

For theſe nocturnal thieves, huntſman, prepare
Thy ſharpeſt vengeance. Oh! how glorious 'tis
To right th' oppreſs'd, and bring the felon vile
To juſt diſgrace! Ere yet the morning peep,
Or ſtars retire from the firſt bluſh of day,
With thy far-echoing voice alarm thy pack,
And rouſe thy bold compeers. Then to the copſe,
Thick with entangling graſs, or prickly furze,
With ſilence lead thy many-colour'd hounds,
In all their beauty's pride. See! how they range
Diſpers'd, how buſily this way, and that,
They croſs, examining with curious noſe
Each likely haunt. Hark! on the drag I hear
Their doubtful notes, preluding to a cry
More nobly full, and ſwell'd with ev'ry mouth.
As ſtraggling armies, at the trumpet's voice,

Preſs

Press to their standard; hither all repair,
And hurry thro' the woods; with hasty step
Rustling, and full of hope; now driv'n on heaps
They push, they strive; while from his kennel sneaks
The conscious villain. See! he skulks along,
Sleek at the shepherd's cost, and plump with meals
Purloin'd. So thrive the wicked here below.
Tho' high his brush he bear, tho' tipt with white
It gaily shine; yet ere the sun declin'd
Recal the shades of night, the pamper'd rogue
Shall rue his fate revers'd; and at his heels
Behold the just avenger, swift to seize
His forfeit head, and thirsting for his blood.

Heavens! what melodious strains! how beat our hearts
Big with tumultuous joy! the loaded gales
Breathe harmony; and as the tempest drives

From wood to wood, thro' ev'ry dark recess
The forest thunders, and the mountains shake.
The chorus swells; less various, and less sweet
The trilling notes, when in those very groves,
The feather'd choristers salute the spring,
And ev'ry bush in concert joins; or when
The master's hand, in modulated air,
Bids the loud organ breathe, and all the pow'rs
Of musick in one instrument combine,
An universal minstrelsy. And now
In vain each earth he tries, the doors are barr'd
Impregnable, nor is the covert safe;
He pants for purer air. Hark! what loud shouts
Re-echo thro' the groves! he breaks away.
Shrill horns proclaim his flight. Each straggling hound
Strains o'er the lawn to reach the distant pack.
'Tis triumph all and joy. Now, my brave youths,
Now give a loose to the clean gen'rous steed;

Flourish

Flourish the whip, nor spare the galling spur;
But in the madness of delight, forget
Your fears. Far o'er the rocky hills we range,
And dangerous our course; but in the brave
True courage never fails. In vain the stream
In foaming eddies whirls; in vain the ditch
Wide-gaping threatens death. The craggy steep
Where the poor dizzy shepherd crawls with care,
And clings to ev'ry twig, gives us no pain;
But down we sweep, as stoops the falcon bold
To pounce his prey. Then up th' opponent hill,
By the swift motion flung, we mount aloft:
So ships in winter-seas now sliding sink
Adown the steepy wave, then toss'd on high
Ride on the billows, and defy the storm.

What lengths we pass! where will the wandring chace
Lead us bewilder'd! smooth as swallows skim

The new-ſhorn mead, and far more ſwift we fly.
See my brave pack; how to the head they preſs,
Joſtling in cloſe array, then more diffuſe
Obliquely wheel, while from their op'ning mouths
The vollied thunder breaks. So when the cranes
Their annual voyage ſteer, with wanton wing
Their figure oft they change, and their loud clang
From cloud to cloud rebounds. How far behind
The hunter-crew, wide-ſtraggling o'er the plain!
The panting courſer now with trembling nerves
Begins to reel; urg'd by the goring ſpur,
Makes many a faint effort: he ſnorts, he foams,
The big round drops run trickling down his ſides,
With ſweat and blood diſtain'd. Look back and view
The ſtrange confuſion of the vale below,
Where ſour vexation reigns; ſee yon poor jade,
In vain th' impatient rider frets and ſwears;
With galling ſpurs harrows his mangled ſides;

He can no more : his stiff unpliant limbs
Rooted in earth, unmov'd and fix'd he stands,
For ev'ry cruel curse returns a groan,
And sobs, and faints, and dies. Who without grief
Can view that pamper'd steed, his master's joy,
His minion, and his daily care, well cloath'd,
Well fed with ev'ry nicer cate ; no cost,
No labour spar'd ; who, when the flying chace
Broke from the copse, without a rival led
The num'rous train : now a sad spectacle
Of pride brought low, and humble insolence,
Drove like a pannier'd ass, and scourg'd along.
While these with loosen'd reins, and dangling heels,
Hang on their reeling palfreys, that scarce bear
Their weights ; another in the treach'rous bog
Lies flound'ring half ingulph'd. What biting thoughts
Torment th' abandon'd crew ! Old age laments
His vigour spent : the tall, plump, brawny youth

Curses his cumb'rous bulk; and envies now
The short Pygmean race, he whom kenn[illegible]
With proud insulting leer. A chosen few
Alone the sport enjoy, nor droop beneath
Their pleasing toils. Here, huntsman, from this height
Observe yon birds of prey; if I can judge,
'Tis there the villain lurks: they hover round
And claim him as their own. Was I not right?
See! there he creeps along; his brush he drags,
And sweeps the mire impure; from his wide jaws
His tongue unmoisten'd hangs; symptoms too sure
Of sudden death. Hah! yet he flies, nor yields
To black despair. But one loose more, and all
His wiles are vain. Hark! thro' yon village now
The rattling clamour rings. The barns, the cots,
And leafless elms return the joyous sounds.
Thro' ev'ry homestall, and thro' ev'ry yard,
His midnight walks, panting, forlorn, he flies;

Thro' ev'ry hole he ſneaks, thro' ev'ry jakes
Plunging he wades beſmear'd, and fondly hopes
In a ſuperior ſtench to loſe his own:
But faithful to the track, th' unerring hounds
With peals of echoing vengeance cloſe purſue.
And now diſtreſs'd, no ſhelt'ring covert near,
Into the hen-rooſt creeps, whoſe walls with gore
Diſtain'd atteſt his guilt. There, villain, there
Expect thy fate deſerv'd. And ſoon from thence
The pack inquiſitive, with clamour loud,
Drag out their trembling prize; and on his blood
With greedy tranſport feaſt. In bolder notes
Each ſounding horn proclaims the felon dead:
And all th' aſſembled village ſhouts for joy.
The farmer, who beholds his mortal foe
Stretch'd at his feet, applauds the glorious deed,
And grateful calls us to a ſhort repaſt:
In the full glaſs the liquid amber ſmiles,
Our native product. And his good old mate

With choiceſt viands heaps the lib'ral board,
To crown our triumphs, and reward our toils.

Here muſt th' inſtructive Muſe (but with reſpect)
Cenſure that num'rous pack, that crowd of ſtate,
With which the vain profuſion of the great
Covers the lawn, and ſhakes the trembling copſe.
Pompous incumbrance! A magnificence
Uſeleſs, vexatious! For the wily fox,
Safe in th' increaſing number of his foes,
Kens well the great advantage; ſlinks behind
And ſlyly creeps thro' the ſame beaten track,
And hunts them ſtep by ſtep: then views, eſcap'd
With inward extaſy, the panting throng
In their own footſteps puzzled, foil'd and loſt.
So when proud Eaſtern kings ſummon to arms
Their gaudy legions, from far diſtant climes,
They flock in crowds, unpeopling half a world;

But when the day of battle calls them forth
To charge the well-train'd foe, a band compact
Of choſen vet'rans; they preſs blindly on,
In heaps confus'd, by their own weapons fall,
A ſmoking carnage ſcatter'd o'er the plain.

Nor hounds alone this noxious brood deſtroy:
The plunder'd warrener full many a wile
Deviſes to entrap his greedy foe,
Fat with nocturnal ſpoils. At cloſe of day,
With ſilence drags his trail; then from the ground
Pares thin the cloſe-graz'd turf, there with nice hand
Covers the latent death, with curious ſprings
Prepar'd to fly at once, whene'er the tread
Of man or beaſt unwarily ſhall preſs
The yielding ſurface. By th' indented ſteel
With gripe tenacious held, the felon grins
And ſtruggles, but in vain: yet oft 'tis known,

When ev'ry art has fail'd, the captive fox
Has shar'd the wounded joint, and with a limb
Compounded for his life. But, if perchance
In the deep pitfall plung'd, there's no escape;
But unrepriev'd he dies, and bleach'd in air,
The jest of clowns, his reeking carcass hangs.

Of these are various kinds; not ev'n the king
Of brutes evades this deep devouring grave:
But by the wily African betray'd,
Heedless of fate, within its gaping jaws
Expires indignant. When the orient beam
With blushes paints the dawn; and all the race
Carnivorous, with blood full-gorg'd, retire
Into their darksom cells, there satiate snore
O'er dripping offals, and the mangled limbs
Of men and beasts; the painful forester
Climbs the high hills, whose proud aspiring tops,
With the tall cedar crown'd, and taper fir,

Assail

Assail the clouds. There 'mong the craggy rocks,
And thickets intricate, trembling he views
His footsteps in the sand; the dismal road
And avenue to death. Hither he calls
His watchful bands; and low into the ground
A pit they sink, full many a fathom deep.
Then in the midst a column high is rear'd,
The butt of some fair tree; upon whose top
A lamb is plac'd, just ravish'd from his dam.
And next a wall they build, with stones and earth
Encircling round, and hiding from all view
The dreadful precipice. Now when the shades
Of night hang low'ring o'er the mountain's brow;
And hunger keen, and pungent thirst of blood,
Rouze up the slothful beast, he shakes his sides,
Slow-rising from his lair, and stretches wide
His rav'nous paws, with recent gore distain'd.
The forests tremble, as he roars aloud,
Impatient to destroy. O'erjoy'd he hears

The bleating innocent, that claims in vain
The ſhepherd's care, and ſeeks with piteous moan
The foodful teat; himſelf, alas! deſign'd
Another's meal. For now the greedy brute
Winds him from far; and leaping o'er the mound
To ſeize his trembling prey, headlong is plung'd
Into the deep abyſs. Proſtrate he lies
Aſtunn'd and impotent. Ah! what avail
Thine eye-balls flaſhing fire, thy length of tail,
That laſhes thy broad ſides, thy jaws beſmear'd
With blood and offals crude, thy ſhaggy mane
The terror of the woods, thy ſtately port,
And bulk enormous, ſince by ſtratagem
Thy ſtrength is foil'd? Unequal is the ſtrife,
When ſov'reign reaſon combats brutal rage.

On diſtant Ethiopia's ſun-burnt coaſts,
The black inhabitants a pitfall frame,
But of a diff'rent kind, and diff'rent uſe.

With slender poles the wide capacious mouth,
And hurdles slight, they close; o'er these is spread
A floor of verdant turf, with all its flow'rs
Smiling delusive, and from strictest search
Concealing the deep grave, that yawns below.
Then boughs of trees they cut, with tempting fruit
Of various kinds surcharg'd; the downy peach,
The clust'ring vine, and of bright golden rind
The fragrant orange. Soon as ev'ning grey
Advances slow, besprinkling all around
With kind refreshing dews the thirsty glebe,
The stately elephant from the close shade
With step majestick strides, eager to taste
The cooler breeze, that from the sea-beat shore
Delightful breathes, or in the limpid stream
To lave his panting sides; joyous he scents
The rich repast, unweeting of the death
That lurks within. And soon he sporting breaks
The brittle boughs, and greedily devours

The fruit delicious. Ah! too dearly bought;
The price is life. For now the treach'rous turf
Trembling gives way; and the unwieldy beast,
Self-sinking, drops into the dark profound.
So when dilated vapours, struggling, heave
Th' incumbent earth; if chance the cavern'd ground
Shrinking subside, and the thin surface yield,
Down sinks at once the pond'rous dome, ingulph'd
With all its tow'rs. Subtle, delusive man!
How various are thy wiles! artful to kill
Thy savage foes, a dull unthinking race!
Fierce from his lair, springs forth the speckled pard,
Thirsting for blood, and eager to destroy;
The huntsman flies, but to his flight alone
Confides not: at convenient distance fix'd,
A polish'd mirrour stops in full career
The furious brute; he there his image views;
Spots against spots with rage improving glow;
Another pard his bristly whiskers curls,

Grins

Grins as he grins, fierce-menacing, and wide
Distends his op'ning paws; himself against
Himself oppos'd, and with dread vengeance arm'd.
The huntsman, now secure, with fatal aim
Directs the pointed spear, by which transfix'd
He dies, and with him dies the rival shade.
Thus man innum'rous engines forms, t'assail
The savage kind; but most the docile horse,
Swift and confederate with man, annoys
His brethren of the plains; without whose aid
The hunter's arts are vain, unskill'd to wage
With the more active brutes an equal war.
But born by him, without the well-train'd pack,
Man dares his foe, on wings of wind secure.

Him the fierce Arab mounts, and, with his troop
Of bold compeers, ranges the deserts wild,
Where, by the magnet's aid, the traveller
Steers his untrodden course; yet oft on land

Is wreck'd, in the high-rolling waves of sand
Immerst and lost. While these intrepid bands,
Safe in their horses speed, out-fly the storm,
And scouring round, make men and beasts their
prey.
The grisly boar is singled from his herd
As large as that in Erimanthian woods,
A match for Hercules. Round him thy fly
In circles wide; and each in passing sends
His feather'd death into his brawny sides.
But perilous th' attempt. For if the steed
Haply too near approach; or the loose earth
His footing fail; the watchful angry beast
Th' advantage spies; and at one sidelong glance
Rips up his groin. Wounded, he rears aloft,
And plunging, from his back the rider hurls
Precipitant; then bleeding spurns the ground,
And drags his reeking entrails o'er the plain.
Mean while the surly monster trots along,

But

But with unequal speed; for still they wound,
Swift-wheeling in the spacious ring. A wood
Of darts upon his back he bears; adown
His tortur'd sides, the crimson torrents roll
From many a gaping font. And now at last
Stagg'ring he falls, in blood and foam expires.

But whither roves my devious muse, intent
On antique tales? While yet the royal stag
Unsung remains. Tread with respectful awe
WINDSOR's green glades; where DENHAM, tuneful bard,
Charm'd once the list'ning dryads, with his song
Sublimely sweet. O! grant me, sacred shade,
To glean submiss what thy full sickle leaves.

THE morning sun, that gilds with trembling rays
WINDSOR's high tow'rs, beholds the courtly train
Mount for the chace, nor views in all his course

A ſcene ſo gay: heroick, noble youths,
In arts and arms renown'd, and lovely nymphs
The faireſt of this iſle, where Beauty dwells
Delighted, and deſerts her Paphian grove
For our more favour'd ſhades: in proud parade
Theſe ſhine magnificent, and preſs around
The royal happy pair. Great in themſelves,
They ſmile ſuperior; of external ſhow
Regardleſs, while their inbred virtues give
A luſtre to their pow'r, and grace their court
With real ſplendors, far above the pomp
Of eaſtern kings, in all their tinſel pride.
Like troops of Amazons, the female band
Prance round their cars, not in refulgent arms
As thoſe of old; unſkill'd to wield the ſword,
Or bend the bow, theſe kill with ſurer aim.
The royal offspring, faireſt of the fair,
Lead on the ſplendid train. Anna more bright
Than ſummer ſuns, or as the light'ning keen,

With irreſiſtible effulgence arm'd,
Fires ev'ry heart. He muſt be more than man,
Who unconcern'd can bear the piercing ray.
Amelia, milder than the bluſhing dawn,
With ſweet engaging air, but equal pow'r,
Inſenſibly ſubdues, and in ſoft chains
Her willing captives leads. Illuſtrious maids
Ever triumphant! whoſe victorious charms,
Without the needleſs aid of high deſcent,
Had aw'd mankind, and taught the world's great
lords
To bow and ſue for grace. But who is he
Freſh as a roſe-bud newly blown, and fair
As op'ning lilies; on whom ev'ry eye
With joy and admiration dwells? See, ſee,
He reins his docile barb with manly grace.
Is it Adonis for the chace array'd?
Or Britain's ſecond hope? Hail blooming youth!
May all your virtues with your years improve,

Till

Till in conſummate worth, you ſhine the pride
Of theſe our days, and to ſucceeding times
A bright example. As his guard of mutes
On the great ſultan wait, with eyes deject
And fix'd on earth, no voice, no ſound is heard
Within the wide ſerail, but all is huſh'd,
And awful ſilence reigns; thus ſtand the pack
Mute and unmov'd, and cow'ring low to earth,
While paſs the glitt'ring court, and royal pair:
So diſciplin'd thoſe hounds, and ſo reſerv'd,
Whoſe honour 'tis to glad the hearts of kings.
But ſoon the winding horn, and huntſman's voice,
Let looſe the gen'ral chorus; far around
Joy ſpreads its wings, and the gay morning ſmiles.

Unharbour'd now the royal ſtag forſakes
His wonted lair; he ſhakes his dappled ſides,
And toſſes high his beamy head, the copſe
Beneath his antlers bends. What doubling ſhifts

He tries !. not more the wily hare; in theſe
Wou'd ſtill perſiſt, did not the full-mouth'd pack
With dreadful conſort thunder in his rear.
The woods reply, the hunter's chearing ſhouts
Float thro' the glades, and the wide foreſt rings.
How merrily they chant! their noſtrils deep
Inhale the grateful ſteam. Such is the cry,
And ſuch th' harmonious din, the ſoldier deems
The battle kindling, and the ſtateſman grave
Forgets his weighty cares; each age, each ſex
In the wild tranſport joins; luxuriant joy,
And pleaſure in exceſs, ſparkling exult
On ev'ry brow, and revel unreſtrain'd.
How happy art thou, man, when thou'rt no more
Thy ſelf! when all the pangs that grind thy ſoul,
In rapture and in ſweet oblivion loſt,
Yield a ſhort interval, and eaſe from pain!

See the ſwift courſer ſtrains, his ſhining hoofs
Securely beat the ſolid ground. Who now
The dang'rous pitfall fears, with tangling heath
High-overgrown? Or who the quiv'ring bog
Soft-yielding to the ſtep? All now is plain,
Plain as the ſtrand ſea-lav'd, that ſtretches far
Beneath the rocky ſhore. Glades croſſing glades
The foreſt opens to our wond'ring view:
Such was the king's command. Let tyrants fierce
Lay waſte the world; his the more glorious part
To check their pride; and when the brazen voice
Of war is huſh'd (as erſt victorious Rome)
T'employ his ſtation'd legions in the works
Of peace; to ſmooth the rugged wilderneſs,
To drain the ſtagnate fen, to raiſe the ſlope
Depending road, and to make gay the face
Of nature, with th' embelliſhments of art.

How melts my beating heart! as I behold
Each lovely nymph, our island's boast and pride,
Push on the gen'rous steed, that strokes along
O'er rough, o'er smooth, nor heeds the steepy hill,
Nor faulters in th' extended vale below:
Their garments loosely waving in the wind,
And all the flush of beauty in their cheeks!
While at their sides their pensive lovers wait,
Direct their dubious course; now chill'd with fear
Solicitous, and now with love inflam'd.
O! grant, indulgent heav'en, no rising storm
May darken, with black wings, this glorious scene!
Shou'd some malignant pow'r thus damp our joys,
Vain were the gloomy cave, such as of old
Betray'd to lawless love the TYRIAN queen.
For BRITAIN's virtuous nymphs are chaste as fair,
Spotless, unblam'd, with equal triumph reign
In the dun gloom, as in the blaze of day.

Now the blown ſtag, thro' woods, bogs, roads,
and ſtreams
Has meaſur'd half the foreſt; but alas!
He flies in vain, he flies not from his fears.
Tho' far he caſt the ling'ring pack behind,
His haggard fancy ſtill with horror views
The fell deſtroyer; ſtill the fatal cry
Inſults his ears, and wounds his trembling heart.
So the poor fury-haunted wretch (his hands
In guiltleſs blood diſtain'd) ſtill ſeems to hear
The dying ſhrieks; and the pale threat'ning ghoſt
Moves as he moves, and as he flies, purſues.
See here his ſlot; up yon green hill he climbs,
Pants on its brow a while, ſadly looks back
On his purſuers, cov'ring all the plain;
Bnt wrung with anguiſh, bears not long the ſight,
Shoots down the ſteep, and ſweats along the vale:
There mingles with the herd, where once he
reign'd

Proud monarch of the groves, whoſe claſhing beam
His rivals aw'd, and whoſe exalted pow'r
Was ſtill rewarded with ſucceſsful love.
But the baſe herd have learn'd the ways of men,
Averſe they fly, or with rebellious aim
Chace him from thence: needleſs their impious
deed,
The huntſman knows him by a thouſand marks,
Black, and imboſt; nor are his hounds deceiv'd;
Too well diſtinguiſh theſe, and never leave
Their once devoted foe; familiar grows
His ſcent, and ſtrong their appetite to kill.
Again he flies, and with redoubled ſpeed
Skims o'er the lawn; ſtill the tenacious crew
Hang on the track, aloud demand their prey,
And puſh him many a league. If haply then
Too far eſcap'd, and the gay courtly train
Behind are caſt, the huntſman's clanging whip
Stops full their bold career; paſſive they ſtand,

Unmov'd, an humble, an obſequious crowd,
As if by ſtern MEDUSA gaz'd to ſtones.
So at their gen'ral's voice whole armies halt
In full purſuit, and check their thirſt of blood.
Soon at the king's command, like haſty ſtreams
Damm'd up a while, they foam, and pour along
With freſh-recruited might. The ſtag, who hop'd
His foes were loſt, now once more hears aſtunn'd
The dreadful din; he ſhivers ev'ry limb,
He ſtarts, he bounds; each buſh preſents a foe.
Preſs'd by the freſh relay, no pauſe allow'd,
Breathleſs, and faint, he faulters in his pace,
And lifts his weary limbs with pain, that ſcarce
Suſtain their load: he pants, he ſobs appall'd;
Drops down his heavy head to earth, beneath
His cumbrous beams oppreſs'd. But if perchance
Some prying eye ſurprize him; ſoon he rears
Erect his tow'ring front, bounds o'er the lawn
With ill-diſſembled vigour, to amuſe

The

The knowing foreſter; who inly ſmiles
At his weak ſhifts, and unavailing frauds.
So midnight tapers waſte their laſt remains,
Shine forth a while, and as they blaze expire.
From wood to wood redoubling thunders roll,
And bellow thro' the vales; the moving ſtorm
Thickens amain, and loud triumphant ſhouts,
And horns ſhrill-warbling in each glade, prelude
To his approaching fate. And now in view
With hobbling gait, and high, exerts amaz'd
What ſtrength is left: to the laſt dregs of life
Reduc'd, his ſpirits fail, on ev'ry ſide
Hemm'd in, beſieg'd; not the leaſt op'ning left
To gleaming hope, th' unhappy's laſt reſerve.
Where ſhall he turn? or whither fly? Deſpair
Gives courage to the weak. Reſolv'd to die,
He fears no more, but ruſhes on his foes,
And deals his deaths around; beneath his feet
Theſe grov'ling lie, thoſe by his antlers gor'd

Defile th' ensanguin'd plain. Ah! see distress'd
He stands at bay against yon knotty trunk,
That covers well his rear, his front presents
An host of foes. O! shun, ye noble train,
The rude encounter, and believe your lives
Your country's due alone. As now aloof
They wing around, he finds his soul uprais'd,
To dare some great exploit; he charges home
Upon the broken pack, that on each side
Fly diverse; then as o'er the turf he strains,
He vents the cooling stream, and up the breeze
Urges his course with eager violence:
Then takes the soil, and plunges in the flood
Precipitant; down the mid-stream he wafts
Along, till (like a ship distress'd, that runs
Into some winding creek) close to the verge
Of a small island, for his weary feet
Sure anchorage he finds, there skulks immers'd.
His nose alone above the wave draws in

The

The vital air; all else beneath the flood
Conceal'd, and lost, deceives each prying eye
Of man or brute. In vain the crowding pack
Draw on the margin of the stream, or cut
The liquid wave with oary feet, that move
In equal time. The gliding waters leave
No trace behind, and his contracted pores
But sparingly perspire: the huntsman strains
His lab'ring lungs, and puffs his cheeks in vain:
At length a blood-hound bold, studious to kill,
And exquisite of sense, winds him from far;
Headlong he leaps into the flood, his mouth
Loud op'ning spends amain, and his wide throat
Swells ev'ry note with joy; then fearless dives
Beneath the wave, hangs on his hanch, and wounds
Th' unhappy brute, that flounders in the stream,
Sorely distress'd, and struggling strives to mount
The steepy shore. Haply once more escap'd,
Again he stands at bay, amid the groves

Of willows, bending low their downy heads.
Outrageous tranſport fires the greedy pack;
Theſe ſwim the deep, and thoſe crawl up with
pain
The ſlippery bank, while others on firm land
Engage; the ſtag repels each bold aſſault,
Maintains his poſt, and wounds for wounds re-
turns.
As when ſome wily corſair boards a ſhip
Full-freighted, or from Afric's golden coaſts,
Or India's wealthy ſtrand, his bloody crew
Upon her deck he flings; theſe in the deep
Drop ſhort, and ſwim to reach her ſteepy ſides,
And clinging climb aloft; while thoſe on board
Urge on the work of fate; the maſter bold,
Preſs'd to his laſt retreat, bravely reſolves
To ſink his wealth beneath the whelming wave,
His wealth, his foes, nor unreveng'd to die.
So fares it with the ſtag: ſo he reſolves

To plunge at once into the flood below,
Himself, his foes in one deep gulph immers'd.
Ere yet he executes this dire intent,
In wild disorder once more views the light;
Beneath a weight of woe, he groans distress'd:
The tears run trickling down his hairy cheeks;
He weeps, nor weeps in vain. The king beholds
His wretched plight, and tenderness innate
Moves his great soul. Soon at his high command
Rebuk'd, the disappointed, hungry pack
Retire submiss, and grumbling quit their prey.

Great Prince! from thee, what may thy subjects hope;
So kind, and so beneficent to brutes?
O mercy, heav'nly born! sweet attribute!
Thou great, thou best prerogative of pow'r!
Justice may guard the throne, but join'd with thee,

On rocks of adamant it ſtands ſecure,
And braves the ſtorm beneath; ſoon as thy ſmiles
Gild the rough deep, the foaming waves ſubſide,
And all the noiſy tumult ſinks in peace.

The ARGUMENT of the Fourth Book.

OF the necessity of destroying some beasts, and preserving others for the use of man. Of breeding of hounds; the season for this business. The choice of the dog, of great moment. Of the litter of whelps. Of the number to be rear'd. Of setting them out to their several walks. Care to be taken to prevent their hunting too soon. Of entering the whelps. Of breaking them from running at sheep. Of the diseases of hounds. Of their age. Of madness; two sorts of it described, the dumb, and outrageous madness: its dreadful effects. Burning of the wound recommended as preventing all ill consequences. The infectious hounds to be separated, and fed apart. The vanity of trusting to the many infallible cures for this malady. The dismal effects of the biting of a mad dog, upon man, described. Description of the otter hunting. The conclusion.

BOOK

BOOK THE FOURTH.

WHATE'ER of earth is form'd, to earth returns
Diſſolv'd; the various objects we behold,
Plants, animals, this whole material maſs,
Are ever changing, ever new. The ſoul
Of man alone, that particle divine,
Eſcapes the wreck of worlds, when all things fail.
Hence great the diſtance 'twixt the beaſts that periſh,
And God's bright image, man's immortal race.
The brute creation are his property,
Subſervient to his will, and for him made.
As hurtful theſe he kills, as uſeful thoſe
Preſerves; their ſole and arbitrary king.

Shou'd he not kill, as erſt the Samian ſage
Taught unadvis'd, and Indian brachmans now
As vainly preach; the teeming rav'nous brutes
Might fill the ſcanty ſpace of this terrene,
Incumb'ring all the globe: ſhou'd not his care
Improve his growing ſtock, their kinds might fail,
Man might once more on roots, and acorns feed,
And thro' the deſerts range, ſhiv'ring, forlorn,
Quite deſtitute of ev'ry ſolace dear,
And ev'ry ſmiling gaiety of life.

The prudent huntſman therefore will ſupply
With annual large recruits, his broken pack,
And propagate their kind. As from the root
Freſh ſcions ſtill ſpring forth, and daily yield
New blooming honours to the parent-tree.
Far ſhall his pack be fam'd, far ſought his breed,
And princes at their tables feaſt thoſe hounds
His hand preſents, an acceptable boon.

Ere yet the Sun thro' the bright Ram has urg'd
His ſteepy courſe, or mother Earth unbound
Her frozen boſom to the WESTERN gale;
When feather'd troops, their ſocial leagues diſ-
ſolv'd,
Select their mates, and on the leafleſs elm
The noiſy rook builds high her wicker neſt,
Mark well the wanton females of thy pack,
That curl their taper tails, and friſking court
Their pyebald mates enamour'd; their red eyes
Flaſh fires impure; nor reſt, nor food they take,
Goaded by furious love. In ſep'rate cells
Confine them now, leſt bloody civil wars
Annoy thy peaceful ſtate. If left at large,
The growling rivals in dread battle join,
And rude encounter; on SCAMANDER's ſtreams
Heroes of old with far leſs fury fought,
For the bright SPARTAN dame, their valour's prize.
Mangled and torn thy fav'rite hounds ſhall lie,

A. Walker del: et Sculp.

... on the ground; thy beard shall appear

... like some ... town

... civil ...

... strange ...

... hands ...

... and ... below ...

... the ... effects of Jewish ...

... long ...

... place ...

Where ... this thing ...

Nor will ... hunt ... regard

Stretch'd on the ground; thy kennel ſhall appear
A field of blood: like ſome unhappy town
In civil broils confus'd, while Diſcord ſhakes
Her bloody ſcourge aloft, fierce parties rage,
Staining their impious hands in mutual death.
And ſtill the beſt belov'd, and braveſt fall:
Such are the dire effects of lawleſs love.

Huntsman! theſe ills by timely prudent care
Prevent: for ev'ry longing dame ſelect
Some happy paramour; to him alone
In leagues connubial join. Conſider well
His lineage; what his fathers did of old,
Chiefs of the pack, and firſt to climb the rock,
Or plung into the deep, or tread the brake
With thorns ſharp-pointed, plaſh'd, and briars inwoven.
Obſerve with care his ſhape, ſort, colour, ſize.
Nor will ſagacious huntſmen leſs regard

His

His inward habits: the vain babbler ſhun,
Ever loquacious, ever in the wrong.
His fooliſh offspring ſhall offend thy ears
With falſe alarms, and loud impertinence.
Nor leſs the ſhifting cur avoid, that breaks
Illuſive from the pack; to the next hedge
Devious he ſtrays, there ev'ry muſe he tries:
If haply then he croſs the ſtreaming ſcent,
Away he flies vain-glorious; and exults
As of the pack ſupreme, and in his ſpeed
And ſtrength unrivall'd. Lo! caſt far behind
His vex'd aſſociates pant, and lab'ring ſtrain
To climb the ſteep aſcent. Soon as they reach
Th' inſulting boaſter, his falſe courage fails,
Behind he lags, doom'd to the fatal nooſe,
His maſter's hate, and ſcorn of all the field.
What can from ſuch be hop'd, but a baſe brood
Of coward curs, a frantick, vagrant race?

WHEN

When now the third revolving moon appears,
With ſharpen'd horns, above the horizon's brink;
Without Lucina's aid, expect thy hopes
Are amply crown'd; ſhort pangs produce to light
The ſmoking litter, crawling, helpleſs, blind,
Nature their guide, they ſeek the pouting teat
That plenteous ſtreams. Soon as the tender dam
Has form'd them with her tongue, with pleaſure view
The marks of their renown'd progenitors,
Sure pledge of triumphs yet to come. All theſe
Select with joy; but to the merc'leſs flood
Expoſe the dwindling refuſe, nor o'erload
Th' indulgent mother. If thy heart relent,
Unwilling to deſtroy, a nurſe provide,
And to the foſter-parent give the care
Of thy ſuperfluous brood; ſhe'll cheriſh kind
The alien offſpring; pleas'd thou ſhalt behold
Her tenderneſs, and hoſpitable love.

If frolick now, and playful they deſert
Their gloomy cell, and on the verdant turf
With nerves improv'd, purſue the mimick chace,
Courſing around; unto the choiceſt friends
Commit thy valu'd prize: the ruſtick dames
Shall at thy kennel wait, and in their laps
Receive thy growing hopes, with many a kiſs
Careſs, and dignify their little charge
With ſome great title, and reſounding name
Of high import. But cautious here obſerve
To check their youthful ardour, nor permit
The unexperienc'd younker, immature,
Alone to range the woods, or haunt the brakes
Where dodging conies ſport: his nerves unſtrung,
And ſtrength unequal; the laborious chace
Shall ſtint his growth, and his raſh forward youth
Contract ſuch vicious habits, as thy care
And late correction never ſhall reclaim.

When to full ſtrength arriv'd, mature and bold,
Conduct them to the field; not all at once,
But as thy cooler prudence ſhall direct,
Select a few, and form them by degrees
To ſtricter diſcipline. With theſe conſort
The ſtanch, and ſteady ſages of thy pack,
By long experience vers'd in all the wiles,
And ſubtle doublings of the various chace.
Eaſy the leſſon of the youthful train,
When inſtinct prompts, and when example guides.
If the too forward younker at the head
Preſs boldly on, in wanton ſportive mood,
Correct his haſte, and let him feel abaſh'd
The ruling whip. But if he ſtoop behind
In wary modeſt guiſe, to his own noſe
Confiding ſure; give him full ſcope to work
His winding way, and with thy voice applaud
His patience, and his care; ſoon ſhalt thou view

The hopeful pupil leader of his tribe,
And all the liſt'ning pack attend his call.

Oft lead them forth where wanton lambkins
play,
And bleating dams with jealous eyes obſerve
Their tender care. If at the crowding flock
He bay preſumptuous, or with eager haſte
Purſue them ſcatter'd o'er the verdant plain;
In the foul fact attach'd, to the ſtrong ram
Tie faſt the raſh offender.—See! at firſt
His horn'd companion, fearful, and amaz'd,
Shall drag him trembling o'er the rugged ground:
Then with his load fatigu'd, ſhall turn a-head,
And with his curl'd hard front inceſſant peal
The panting wretch; till breathleſs and aſtunn'd,
Stretch'd on the turf he lie. Then ſpare not thou
The twining whip, but ply his bleeding ſides

Laſh after laſh, and with thy threat'ning voice,
Harſh-echoing from the hills, inculcate loud
His vile offence. Sooner ſhall trembling doves
Eſcap'd the hawk's ſharp talons, in mid air,
Aſſail the dang'rous foe, than he once more
Diſturb the peaceful flocks. In tender age
Thus youth is train'd; as curious artiſts bend
The taper, pliant twig: or potters form
Their ſoft and ductile clay to various ſhapes.

Nor is 't enough to breed; but to preſerve
Muſt be the huntſman's care. The ſtanch old hounds,
Guides of thy pack, tho' but in number few,
Are yet of great account; ſhall oft untye
The Gordian knot, when reaſon at a ſtand
Puzzling is loſt, and all thy art is vain,
O'er clogging fallows, o'er dry plaſter'd roads,
O'er floated meads, o'er plains with flocks diſtain'd

Rank-ſcenting, theſe muſt lead the dubious way.
As party-chiefs in ſenates who preſide,
With pleaded reaſon and with well-turn'd ſpeech,
Conduct the ſtaring multitude; ſo theſe
Direct the pack, who with joint cry approve,
And loudly boaſt diſcov'ries not their own.

Unnumber'd accidents, and various ills,
Attend thy pack, hang hov'ring o'er their heads,
And point the way that leads to Death's dark cave.
Short is their ſpan; few at the date arrive
Of ancient Argus in old Homer's ſong
So highly honour'd: kind, ſagacious brute!
Not ev'n Minerva's wiſdom could conceal
Thy much lov'd maſter from thy nicer ſenſe.
Dying his lord he own'd, view'd him all o'er
With eager eyes, then clos'd thoſe eyes, well pleas'd,

Of leſſer ills the muſe declines to ſing,
Nor ſtoops ſo low; of theſe each groom can tell
The proper remedy. But O! what care!
What prudence can prevent madneſs, the worſt
Of maladies? Terrifick peſt! that blaſts
The huntſman's hopes, and deſolation ſpreads
Thro' all th' unpeopled kennel unreſtrain'd,
More fatal than th' envenom'd viper's bite;
Or that Apulian ſpider's pois'nous ſting,
Heal'd by the pleaſing antidote of ſounds.

When Sirius reigns, and the ſun's parching
beams
Bake the dry gaping ſurface, viſit thou
Each ev'n and morn, with quick obſervant eye,
Thy panting pack. If in dark ſullen mood,
The glouting hound refuſe his wonted meal,
Retiring to ſome cloſe, obſcure retreat,
Gloomy, diſconſolate: with ſpeed remove

The poor infectious wretch, and in ſtrong chains
Bind him ſuſpected. Thus that dire diſeaſe
Which art can't cure, wiſe caution may prevent.

But this neglected, ſoon expect a change,
A diſmal change, confuſion, frenzy, death.
Or in ſome dark receſs the ſenſeleſs brute
Sits ſadly pining: deep melancholy,
And black deſpair, upon his clouded brow
Hang low'ring; from his half-op'ning jaws
The clammy venom, and infectious froth,
Diſtilling fall; and from his lungs inflam'd,
Malignant vapours taint the ambient air,
Breathing perdition: his dim eyes are glaz'd,
He droops his penſive head, his trembling limbs
No more ſupport his weight; abject he lies,
Dumb, ſpiritleſs, benumb'd; till death at laſt
Gracious attends, and kindly brings relief.

Or if outrageous grown, behold, alas!
A yet more dreadful scene; his glaring eyes
Redden with fury, like some angry boar
Churning he foams; and on his back erect
His pointed bristles rise; his tail incurv'd
He drops, and with harsh broken howlings rends
The poison-tainted air, with rough hoarse voice
Incessant bays; and snuffs th' infectious breeze;
This way and that he stares aghast, and starts
At his own shade: jealous, as if he deem'd
The world his foes. If haply tow'rds the stream
He cast his roving eye, cold horror chills
His soul; averse he flies, trembling, appall'd.
Now frantick to the kennel's utmost verge
Raving he runs, and deals destruction round.
The pack fly diverse; for whate'er he meets
Vengeful he bites, and ev'ry bite is death.

If now perchance thro' the weak fence escap'd,
Far up the wind he roves, with open mouth

Inhales the cooling breeze, nor man, nor beaſt
He ſpares implacable. The hunter-horſe,
Once kind aſſociate of his ſylvan toils,
(Who haply now without the kennel's mound
Crops the rank mead, and liſt'ning hears with joy
The chearing cry, that morn and eve ſalutes
His raptur'd ſenſe) a wretched victim falls.
Unhappy quadruped! no more, alas!
Shall thy fond maſter with his voice applaud
Thy gentleneſs, thy ſpeed; or with his hand
Stroke thy ſoft dappled ſides, as he each day
Viſits thy ſtall, well pleas'd; no more ſhalt thou
With ſprightly neighings, to the winding horn,
And the loud op'ning pack in concert join'd,
Glad his proud heart. For oh! the ſecret wound
Rankling inflames, he bites the ground and dies.

Hence to the village with pernicious haſte
Baleful he bends his courſe: the village flies

Alarm'd;

Alarm'd; the tender mother in her arms
Hugs cloſe the trembling babe; the doors are barr'd,
And flying curs by native inſtinct taught
Shun the contagious bane; the ruſtick bands
Hurry to arms, the rude militia ſeize
Whate'er at hand they find; clubs, forks, or guns
From ev'ry quarter charge the furious foe,
In wild diſcorder, and uncouth array:
Till now with wounds on wounds oppreſſ'd and gor'd,
At one ſhort pois'nous gaſp he breathes his laſt.

Hence to the kennel, Muſe, return, and view
With heavy heart that hoſpital of woe;
Where Horror ſtalks at large; inſatiate Death
Sits growling o'er his prey: each hour preſents
A diff'rent ſcene of ruin and diſtreſs.
How buſy art thou, Fate! and how ſevere

Thy pointed wrath! the dying and the dead
Promiscuous lie; o'er these the living fight
In one eternal broil; not conscious why,
Nor yet with whom. So drunkards, in their cups,
Spare not their friends, while senseless squabble reigns.

Huntsman! it much behoves thee to avoid
The perilous debate! Ah! rouze up all
Thy vigilance, and tread the treach'rous ground
With careful step. Thy fires unquench'd preserve,
As erst the vestal flames; the pointed steel
In the hot embers hide; and if surpriz'd
Thou feel'st the deadly bite, quick urge it home
Into the recent sore, and cauterize
The wound; spare not thy flesh, nor dread th' event:
Vulcan shall save when Æsculapius fails.

Here ſhou'd the knowing Muſe recount the means
To ſtop this growing plague. And here, alas!
Each hand preſents a ſov'reign cure, and boaſts
Infallibility, but boaſts in vain.
On this depend, each to his ſep'rate ſeat
Confine, in fetters bound; give each his meſs
Apart, his range in open air; and then
If deadly ſymptoms to thy grief appear,
Devote the wretch, and let him greatly fall,
A gen'rous victim for the publick weal.

Sing, philoſophick Muſe, the dire effects
Of this contagious bite on hapleſs man.
The ruſtick ſwains, by long tradition taught
Of leaches old, as ſoon as they perceive
The bite impreſs'd, to the ſea-coaſts repair.
Plung'd in the briny flood, th' unhappy youth
Now journeys home ſecure; but ſoon ſhall wiſh

The

The ſeas as yet had cover'd him beneath
The foaming ſurge, full many a fathom deep.
A fate more diſmal, and ſuperior ills
Hang o'er his head devoted. When the moon,
Cloſing her monthly round, returns again
To glad the night; or when full-orb'd ſhe ſhines,
High in the vault of heav'n; the lurking peſt
Begins the dire aſſault. The pois'nous foam
Thro' the deep wound inſtill'd with hoſtile rage,
And all its fiery particles ſaline,
Invades th' arterial fluid: whoſe red waves
Tempeſtuous heave, and their coheſion broke,
Fermenting boil; inteſtine war enſues,
And order to confuſion turns embroil'd.
Now the diſtended veſſels ſcarce contain
The wild uproar, but preſs each weaker part,
Unable to reſiſt: the tender brain
And ſtomach ſuffer moſt; convulſions ſhake
His trembling nerves, and wand'ring pungent pains

Pinch sore the sleepless wretch; his flutt'ring pulse
Oft intermits; pensive, and sad, he mourns
His cruel fate, and to his weeping friends
Laments in vain; to hasty anger prone,
Resents each slight offence, walks with quick step,
And wildly stares; at last with boundless sway
The tyrant frenzy reigns. For as the dog
(Whose fatal bite convey'd th' infectious bane)
Raving he foams, and howls and barks, and bates.
Like agitations in his boiling blood
Present like species to his troubled mind;
His nature, and his actions all canine.
So (as old HOMER sung) th' associates wild
Of wand'ring ITHACUS, by CIRCE's charms
To swine transform'd, ran gruntling thro' the groves,
Dreadful example to a wicked world!
See there distress'd he lies! parch'd up with thirst,
But dares not drink. Till now at last his soul

Trembling escapes, her noisome dungeon leaves,
And to some purer region wings away.

One labour yet remains, celestial Maid!
Another element demands thy song.
No more o'er craggy steep, thro' coverts thick
With pointed thorn, and briers intricate,
Urge on with horn and voice the painful pack:
But skim with wanton wing th' irriguous vale,
Where winding streams amid the flow'ry meads
Perpetual glide along; and undermine
The cavern'd banks, by the tenacious roots
Of hoary willows arch'd; gloomy retreat
Of the bright scaly kind; where they at will
On the green watry reed their pasture graze,
Suck the moist soil, or slumber at their ease,
Rock'd by the restless brook, that draws aslope
Its humid train, and laves their dark abodes.
Where rages not oppression? Where, alas!

Is innocence ſecure? Rapine and ſpoil
Haunt ev'n the loweſt deeps; ſeas have their ſharks,
Rivers and ponds inclos'd the rav'nous pike;
He in his turn becomes a prey; on him
Th' amphibious otter feaſts. Juſt is his fate
Deſerv'd: but tyrants know no bounds; nor ſpears
That briſtle on his back, defend the perch
From his wide greedy jaws; nor burniſh'd mail
The yellow carp, nor all his arts can ſave
Th' inſinuating eel, that hides his head
Beneath the ſlimy mud; nor yet eſcapes
The crimſon-ſpotted trout, the river's pride
And beauty of the ſtream. Without remorſe,
This midnight pillager, ranging around,
Inſatiate ſwallows all. The owner mourns
Th' unpeopled rivulet, and gladly hears
The huntſman's early call, and ſees with joy
The jovial crew, that march upon its banks
In gay parade, with bearded lances arm'd.

This subtle spoiler of the beaver kind,
Far off perhaps, where ancient alders shade
The deep still pool; within some hollow trunk
Contrives his wicker couch: whence he surveys
His long purlieu, lord of the stream, and all
The finny shoals his own. But you, brave youths,
Dispute the felon's claim; try ev'ry root,
And ev'ry reedy bank; encourage all
The busy-spreading pack, that fearless plunge
Into the flood, and cross the rapid stream.
Bid rocks and caves, and each resounding shore,
Proclaim your bold defiance; loudly raise
Each chearing voice, till distant hills repeat
The triumphs of the vale. On the soft sand
See there his seal impress'd! and on that bank
Behold the glittering spoils, half-eaten fish,
Scales, fins, and bones, the leavings of his feast.
Ah! on that yielding sag-bed, see once more
His seal I view. O'er yon dank rushy marsh

The

The ſly gooſe-footed prowler bends his courſe,
And ſeeks the diſtant ſhallows. Huntſman, bring
Thy eager pack; and trail him to his couch.
Hark! the loud peal begins, the clam'rous joy,
The gallant chiding, loads the trembling air.

Ye Naiads fair, who o'er theſe floods preſide,
Raiſe up your dripping heads above the wave,
And hear our melody. Th' harmonious notes
Float with the ſtream; and ev'ry winding creek
And hollow rock, that o'er the dimpling flood
Nods pendant; ſtill improve from ſhore to ſhore
Our ſweet reiterated joys. What ſhouts!
What clamour loud! What gay heart-chearing ſounds
Urge thro' the breathing braſs their mazy way!
Nor quires of Tritons glad with ſprightlier ſtrains
The dancing billows! when proud Neptune rides
In triumph o'er the deep. How greedily

They ſnuff the fiſhy ſteam, that to each blade
Rank-ſcenting clings! See! how the morning dews
They ſweep, that from their feet beſprinkling drop
Diſpers'd, and leave a track oblique behind.
Now on firm land they range; then in the flood
They plunge tumultuous; or thro' reedy pools
Ruſtling they work their way: no holt eſcapes
Their curious ſearch. With quick ſenſation now
The fuming vapour ſtings; flutter their hearts,
And joy redoubled burſts from ev'ry mouth
In louder ſymphonies. Yon hollow trunk,
That with its hoary head incurv'd ſalutes
The paſſing wave, muſt be the tyrant's fort,
And dread abode. How theſe impatient climb,
While others at the root inceſſant bay!
They put him down. See, there he dives along!
Th' aſcending bubbles mark his gloomy way.
Quick fix the nets, and cut off his retreat
Into the ſhelt'ring deeps. Ah, there he vents!

The pack lunge headlong, and protended ſpears
Menace deſtruction: while the troubled ſurge
Indignant foams, and all the ſcaly kind,
Affrighted, hide their heads. Wild tumult reigns,
And loud uproar. Ah, there once more he vents!
See, that bold hound has ſeiz'd him; down they ſink
Together loſt: but ſoon ſhall he repent
His raſh aſſault. See there eſcap'd, he flies
Half-drown'd, and clambers up the ſlipp'ry bank
With ouze and blood diſtain'd. Of all the brutes,
Whether by Nature form'd, or by long uſe,
This artful diver beſt can bear the want
Of vital air. Unequal is the fight,
Beneath the whelming element. Yet there
He lives not long; but reſpiration needs
At proper intervals. Again he vents;
Again the crowd attack. That ſpear has pierc'd
His neck; the crimſon waves confeſs the wound.
Fix'd is the bearded lance, unwelcome gueſt,

Where'er he flies; with him it ſinks beneath,
With him it mounts; ſure guide to ev'ry foe.
Inly he groans; nor can his tender wound
Bear the cold ſtream. Lo! to yon ſedgy bank
He creeps diſconſolate: his num'rous foes
Surround him, hounds, and men. Pierc'd thro' and thro',
On pointed ſpears they lift him high in air;
Wriggling he hangs, and grins, and bites in vain:
Bid the loud horns, in gayly-warbling ſtrains,
Proclaim the felon's fate; he dies, he dies.

Rejoice, ye ſcaly tribes, and leaping dance
Above the wave, in ſign of liberty
Reſtor'd; the cruel tyrant is no more.
Rejoice ſecure and bleſs'd; did not as yet
Remain, ſome of your own rapacious kind;
And man, fierce man, with all his various wiles.

Book 4th. page 124.

A. Walker del. et Sculp.

O HAPPY! if ye knew your happy ſtate,
Ye rangers of the fields; whom Nature boon
Chears with her ſmiles, and ev'ry element
Conſpires to bleſs. What, if no heroes frown
From marble pedeſtals; nor RAPHAEL's works,
Nor TITIAN's lively tints, adorn our walls?
Yet theſe the meaneſt of us may behold;
And at another's coſt may feaſt at will
Our wond'ring eyes; what can the owner more?
But vain, alas! is wealth, not grac'd with pow'r.
The flow'ry landſkip, and the gilded dome,
And viſtas op'ning to the wearied eye,
Thro' all his wide domain; the planted grove,
The ſhrubby wilderneſs, with its gay choir
Of warbling birds, can't lull to ſoft repoſe
Th' ambitious wretch, whoſe diſcontented ſoul
Is harrow'd day and night; he mourns, he pines,
Until his prince's favour makes him great.
See there he comes, th' exalted idol comes!

The circle's form'd, and all his fawning ſlaves
Devoutly bow to earth; from ev'ry mouth
The nauſeous flatt'ry flows, which he returns
With promiſes, that die as ſoon as born.
Vile intercourſe! where virtue has no place.
Frown but the monarch; all his glories fade;
He mingles with the throng, outcaſt, undone,
The pageant of a day; without one friend
To ſooth his tortur'd mind; all, all are fled,
For tho' they baſk'd in his meridian ray,
The inſects vaniſh, as his beams decline.

NOT ſuch our friends; for here no dark deſign,
No wicked int'reſt bribes the venal heart;
But inclination to our boſom leads,
And weds them there for life; our ſocial cups
Smile, as we ſmile; open, and unreſerv'd,
We ſpeak our inmoſt ſouls; good humour, mirth,
Soft complaiſance, and wit from malice free,
Smooth ev'ry brow, and glow on ev'ry cheek.

O HAP-

O HAPPINESS sincere! what wretch wou'd groan
Beneath the galling load of pow'r, or walk
Upon the slipp'ry pavements of the great,
Who thus cou'd reign, unenvy'd and secure?

Ye guardian pow'rs who make mankind your care,
Give me to know wise nature's hidden depths,
Trace each mysterious cause, with judgment read
Th' expanded volume, and submiss adore
That great creative Will, who at a word
Spoke forth the wond'rous scene. But if my soul
To this gross clay confin'd flutters on earth
With less ambitious wing; unskill'd to range
From orb to orb, where NEWTON leads the way;
And view with piercing eyes, the grand machine,
Worlds above worlds; subservient to his voice,
Who, veil'd in clouded Majesty, alone
Gives light to all; bids the great system move,

And changeful ſeaſons in their turns advance,
Unmov'd, unchang'd, himſelf. Yet this at leaſt
Grant me propitious, an inglorious life,
Calm and ſerene; nor loſt in falſe purſuits
Of wealth or honours; but enough to raiſe
My drooping friends, preventing modeſt Want
That dares not aſk. And if to crown my joys,
Ye grant me health, that, ruddy in my cheeks,
Blooms in my life's decline; fields, woods, and ſtreams,
Each tow'ring hill, each humble vale below,
Shall hear my chearing voice, my hounds ſhall wake
The lazy morn, and glad th' horizon round.

THE END.

HOBBINOL,

OR THE

RURAL GAMES.

A

BURLESQUE POEM.

IN BLANK VERSE.

By WILLIAM SOMERVILE, Esq.

THE SIXTH EDITION.

Nec sum animi dubius, verbis ea vincere magnum
Quàm sit, et angustis hunc addere rebus honorem.
Sed me Parnassi deserta per ardua dulcis
Raptat Amor. Juvat ire jugis, quà nulla priorum
Castaliam molli divertitur orbita clivo.

VIRG. GEORG. Lib. III.

LONDON:
Printed for W. BOWYER, W. STRAHAN,
and R. BALDWIN. MDCCLXXIII.

DE TION

TO

Mr. HOGARTH.

PERM me, Sir, to make choice of you for my Patron, being the greatest ma ter in the burlesque way. Indeed you have the adv of your poetical brethren. you paint to the eye; member, Sir, that we give speech and motion, and a greater variety to our figures. Your province is the Town; leave me a small our ride in the Country, and I shall be

DEDICATION

TO

Mr. HOGARTH.

PERMIT me, Sir, to make choice of you for my Patron, being the greateſt maſter in the burleſque way. In this indeed you have ſome advantage of your poetical brethren, that you paint to the eye; yet remember, Sir, that we give ſpeech and motion, and a greater variety to our figures. Your province is the Town; leave me a ſmall outride in the Country, and I ſhall be be content. In this, at leaſt, let us both agree, to make vice and folly the object of our ridicule; and we cannot fail to be of ſome ſervice to mankind. I am,

SIR,

Your admirer, and

Moſt humble ſervant,

W. S.

THE

PREFACE.

NOTHING is more common than for us poor bards, when we have acquired a little reputation, to print ourſelves into diſgrace. We climb the AONIAN mount with difficulty and toil; we receive the bays for which we languiſhed; till, graſping ſtill at more, we loſe our hold, and fall at once to the bottom.

THE Author of this piece would not thus be *felo de ſe*, nor would he be murdered by perſons unknown. But as he is ſatisfied, that there are many imperfect copies of this trifle diſperſed abroad, and as he is credibly informed, that he ſhall ſoon be expoſed to view in ſuch an attitude, as he would not care to appear in; he thinks it moſt prudent in this deſperate caſe to throw himſelf on the mercy of the publick; and offer this whimſical

ſical work a voluntary ſacrifice, in hope that he ſtands a better chance for their indulgence, now it has received his laſt hand, than when curtailed and mangled by others.

The Poets of almoſt all nations have celebrated the games of their ſeveral countries. Homer began, and all the mimic tribe followed the example of that great father of poetry. Even our own Milton, who laid his ſcene beyond the limits of this ſublunary world, has found room for deſcriptions of this ſort, and has performed it in a more ſublime manner, than any who went before him. His, indeed, are ſports; but they are the ſports of angels. This gentleman has endeavoured to do juſtice to his countrymen, the British freeholders, who, when dreſſed in their holiday clothes, are by no means perſons of a deſpicable figure; but eat and drink as plentifully, and fight as heartily, as the greateſt hero in the Iliad. There is alſo ſome uſe in deſcriptions of this nature, ſince nothing gives us a clearer idea of the genius of a nation, than their ſports and diverſions. If we ſee people dancing, even in wooden ſhoes, and a fiddle always at their heels, we are ſoon

con-

convinced of the levity and volatile ſpirit of thoſe merry ſlaves. The famous bull feaſts are an evident token of the Quixotiſm and romantic taſte of the SPANIARDS. And a country-wake is too ſad an image of the infirmities of our own people: we ſee nothing but broken heads, bottles flying about, tables overturned, outrageous drunkenneſs, and eternal ſquabble.

THUS much of the ſubject; it may not be improper to touch a little upon the ſtyle. One of the greateſt poets and moſt candid critics of this ages has informed us that there are two ſorts of burleſque. Be pleaſed to take it in his own words, SPECTATOR, Numb. 242. "Burleſque (ſays he) is of two kinds. The "firſt repreſents mean perſons in the accou-"trements of heroes; the other, great per-"ſons acting and ſpeaking like the baſeſt "among the people. Don QUIXOTE is an in-"ſtance of the firſt, and LUCIAN's Gods of "the ſecond. It is a diſpute among the cri-"tics, whether burleſque runs beſt in he-"roic, like the DISPENSARY; or in dog-"grel, like that of HUDIBRAS. I think "where the low character is to be raiſed, "the heroic is the most proper measure; "but when an hero is to be pulled down "and degraded, it is best done in doggrel." Thus far Mr. ADDISON. If therefore the heroic is the proper measure, where the low character is to be raised, MILTON's style must be very proper in the subject here treated of; because it raises the low character more than is possible to be done under the restraint of rhyme; and the ridicule chiefly consists in raising that low character. I beg leave to add the authority of Mr. SMITH, in his poem upon the death of Mr. JOHN PHILIPS. The whole passage is so very fine, and gives so clear an idea of his manner of writing that the reader will not think his labour lost in running it over:

OH various bard! you all our pow'rs controul,
You now disturb, and now divert the soul.
MILTON and BUTLER in thy Muse combine;
Above the last thy manly beauties shine.
For as I've seen two rival wits contend,
One gayly charge, one gravely wise defend;
That on quick turns, and points in vain relies:
This with a look demure, and steady eyes,
With dry rebukes and sneering praise replies:
So thy grave lines extort a juster smile,
Reach BUTLER's fancy, but surpass his style.

He

He ſpeaks SCARRON's low phraſe in humble ſtrains;
In thee the ſolemn air of great CERVANTES reigns.
What ſounding lines his abject themes expreſs!
What ſhining words the pompous SHILLING dreſs!
There, there my cell, immortal made, outvies
The frailer piles, that o'er its ruins riſe.
In her beſt light the comic Muſe appears,
When ſhe with borrow'd pride the buſkin wears.
So when nurſe NOKES to act young AMMON tries,
With ſhambling legs, long chin, and fooliſh eyes,
With dangling hands he ſtrokes th' imperial robe,
And with a cuckold's air commands the globe.
The pomp, and ſound, the whole buffoon diſplay'd,
And AMMON's ſon more mirth than GOMEZ made.

BUT here it may be objected, that this manner of writing contradicts the rule in HORACE:

Verſibus exponi tragicis res comica non vult.

MONSIEUR BOILEAU, in his diſſertation upon the JOCONDE of DE LA FONTAINE, quotes this paſſage in HORACE, and obſerves, *Que comme il n'y a rien de plus froid, que de conter une choſe grande en ſtile bas, auſſi n'y a-t-il de plus ridicule, que de raconter une hiſtoire comique et abſurde en termes graves et ſerieux.* But then he juſtly adds this exception to the general rule in HORACE; *à moins que ce serieux ne soit affecté tout exprés pour rendre la chose encore plus burlesque.* If the observation of that celebrated critic, Monsieur DACIER, is true, HORACE himself, in the same Epistle to the Piso's, and not far distant from the rule here mentioned, has aimed to improve the burlesque by the help of the sublime, in his note upon this verse:

> *Debemur morti nos, nostraque; sive receptus*
> *Terrâ Neptunus* ——

And upon the five following verses has this general remark: *Toutes ces expressions nobles qu'* HORACE *entasse dans ces six vers servent à rendre plus plaisante cette chute:*

> *Ne dum verborum stet honos.*——

Car rien ne contribue tant au ridicule *que le grand.* He indeed would be severe upon himself alone, who should censure this way of writing, when he must plainly see, that it is affected on purpose, only to raise the ridicule, and give the reader a more agreeable enter-

entertainment. Nothing can improve a merry tale so much, as its being delivered with a grave and serious air. Our imaginations are agreeably surprised, and fond of a pleasure so little expected. Whereas he, who would bespeak our laughter by an affected grimace and ridiculous gestures, must play his part very well indeed, or he will fall short of the idea he has raised. It is true, VIRGIL was very sensible that it was difficult thus to elevate a low and mean subject:

Nec sum animi dubius, verbis ea vincere magnum
Quam sit, et angustis hunc addere rebus honorem.

But tells us for our encouragement in another place,

In tenui labor, at tenuis non gloria, siquem
Numina læva sinunt, auditque vocatus APOLLO.

Mr. ADDISON is of the same opinion, and adds, that the difficulty is very much increased by writing in blank verse. "The "ENGLISH and FRENCH, (says he) who always use the same words in verse as in "ordinary conversation, are forced to raise

" their language with metaphors and figures, " or by the pompousness of the whole " phrase to wear off any littleness, that ap- " pears in the particular parts that compose " it. This makes our blank verse, where " there is no rhyme to support the expres- " sion, extremely difficult to such as are " not masters of the tongue; especially " when they write upon *low subjects*." REMARKS UPON ITALY, p. 99. But there is even yet a greater difficulty behind: the writer in this kind of burlesque must not only keep up the pomp and dignity of the style, but an artful sneer should appear through the whole work; and every man will judge, that it is no easy matter to blend together the HERO and HARLEQUIN.

If any person should want a key to this poem, his curiosity shall be gratified: I shall, in plain words, tell him, " It is a sa- " tire against the luxury, the pride, the " wantonness, and quarrelsome temper of " the middling sort of people." As these are the proper and genuine cause of that bare-faced knavery, and almost universal poverty, which reign without controul in every place; and as to these we owe our many bankrupt farmers, our trade decayed, and lands uncultivated; the author has reason to hope that no honest man, who loves his country, will think this short reproof out of season: for, perhaps, this merry way of bantering men into virtue, may have a better effect than the most serious admonitions; since many, who are proud to be thought immoral, are not very fond of being ridiculous.

ARGUMENT of the First CANTO.

PROPOSITION. Invocation addressed to Mr. JOHN PHILLIPS *author of the* CYDER POEM *and* SPLENDID SHILLING. *Description of the Vale of* EVESHAM. *The seat of* HOBBINOL; HOBBINOL *a great man in his village, seated in his wicker smoking his pipe, has one only son. Young* HOBBINOL'*s education, bred up with* GANDERETTA *his near relation. Young* HOBBINOL *and* GANDERETTA *chosen king and queen of* MAY. *Her dress and attendants. The* MAY-GAMES. TWANGDILLO *the fidler, his character. The dancing.* GANDERETTA'*s extraordinary performance. Bagpipes good music in the* HIGHLANDS. MILONIDES *master of the ring, disciplines the mob; proclaims the several prizes. His speech.* PASTOREL *takes up his belt. His character, his heroic figure, his confidence.* HOBBINOL, *by permission of* GANDERETTA, *accepts the challenge, vaults into the ring. His honourable behaviour, escapes a scowering.* GANDERETTA'*s agony.* PASTOREL *foiled.* GANDERETTA *not a little pleased.*

HOBBINOL,

OR THE

RURAL GAMES.

CANTO I.

WHAT old MENALCAS at his feast reveal'd
I sing, strange feats of antient prowess, deeds
Of high renown, while all his list'ning guests
With eager joy receiv'd the pleasing tale.

O THOU *! who late on VAGA's flowery banks
Slumb'ring secure, with STIROM † well bedew'd,
Fallacious cask, in sacred dreams wert taught
By antient seers, and MERLIN prophet old,
To raise ignoble themes with strains sublime,
Be thou my guide! while I thy track pursue

* Mr. JOHN PHILIPS, author of the CYDER-POEM.
† Strong HEREFORDSHIRE CYDER.

With

With wing unequal, thro' the wide expanſe
Advent'rous range, and emulate thy flights.

In that rich vale *, where with DOBUNIAN † fields
CORNAVIAN ‡ borders meet, far-fam'd of old
For MONTFORT'S || hapleſs fate, undaunted earl;
Where from her fruitful urn AVONA pours
Her kindly torrent on the thirſty glebe,
And pillages the hills t' enrich the plains;
On whoſe luxuriant banks flow'rs of all hues
Start up ſpontaneous; and the teeming ſoil
With haſty ſhoots prevents its owner's pray'r:
The pamper'd wanton ſteer, of the ſharp ax
Regardleſs, that o'er his devoted head
Hangs menacing, crops his delicious bane,
Nor knows the price is life; with envious eye
His lab'ring yoke-fellow beholds his plight,

* Vale of EVESHAM. † GLOCESTERSHIRE. ‡ WORCESTERSHIRE. || SIMON DE MONTFORT, killed at the battle of EVESHAM.

And

And deems him bleſt, while on his languid neck
In ſolemn ſloth he tugs the ling'ring plough.
So blind are mortals, of each other's ſtate
Mis-judging, ſelf-deceiv'd. Here as ſupreme
Stern HOBBINOL in rural plenty reigns
O'er wide-extended fields, his large domain.
Th' obſequious villagers, with looks ſubmiſs
Obſervant of his eye, or when with ſeed
T' impregnate Earth's fat womb, or when to bring
With clam'rous joy the bearded harveſt home.

HERE, when the diſtant ſun lengthens the nights,
When the keen froſts the ſhiv'ring farmer warn
To broach his mellow caſk, and frequent blaſts
Inſtruct the crackling billets how to blaze,
In his warm wicker-chair, whoſe pliant twigs
In cloſe embraces join'd, with ſpacious arch
Vault this thick-woven roof, the bloated churl
Loiters in ſtate, each arm reclin'd is prop'd
With yielding pillows of the ſofteſt down.

In mind compos'd, from ſhort coeval tube
He ſucks the vapours bland, thick curling clouds
Of ſmoke around his reeking temples play;
Joyous he ſits, and impotent of thought
Puffs away care, and ſorrow from his heart.
How vain the pomp of kings! Look down, ye great,
And view with envious eye the downy neſt,
Where ſoft Repoſe, and calm Contentment dwell,
Unbrib'd by wealth, and unreſtrain'd by pow'r.

ONE ſon alone had bleſt his bridal bed,
Whom good CALISTA bore, nor long ſurviv'd
To ſhare a mother's joy, but left the babe
To his paternal care. An orphan niece
Near the ſame time his dying brother ſent,
To claim his kind ſupport. The helpleſs pair
In the ſame cradle ſlept, nurs'd up with care
By the ſame tender hand, on the ſame breaſts
Alternate hung with joy; till reaſon dawn'd,
And a new light broke out by ſlow degrees:

Then

Then on the floor the pretty wantons play'd,
Gladding the farmer's heart with growing hopes,
And pleasures erst unfelt. Whene'er with cares
Oppress'd, when wearied, or alone he doz'd,
Their harmless prattle sooth'd his troubled soul.
Say, HOBBINOL, what extasies of joy
Trill'd thro' thy veins, when climbing for a kiss
With little palms they strok'd thy grizly beard,
Or round thy wicker whirl'd their ratt'ling cars?
Thus from their earliest days bred up, and train'd,
To mutual fondness, with their stature grew
The thriving passion. What love can decay
That roots so deep! Now rip'ning manhood curl'd
On the gay stripling's chin: her panting breasts,
And trembling blushes glowing on her cheeks
Her secret wish betray'd. She at each mart
All eyes attracted; but her faithful shade,
Young HOBBINOL, ne'er wander'd from her side.
A frown from him dash'd ev'ry rival's hopes.
For he, like PELEUS son, was prone to rage,

Inexorable

Inexorable, swift like him of foot
With ease cou'd overtake his dastard foe,
Nor spar'd the suppliant wretch. And now approach'd
Those merry days, when all the nymphs and swains,
In solemn festivals and rural sports,
Pay their glad homage to the blooming spring.
Young HOBBINOL by joint consent is rais'd
T' imperial dignity, and in his hand
Bright GANDERETTA tripp'd the jovial queen
Of MAIA's gaudy month profuse of flow'rs.
From each enamel'd mead th' attendant nymphs
Loaded with od'rous spoils, from these select
Each flow'r of gorgeous dye, and garlands weave
Of party-colour'd sweets; each busy hand
Adorns the jocund queen: in her loose hair,
That to the winds in wanton ringlets plays,
The tufted COWSLIPS breathe their faint perfumes.
On her refulgent brow, as crystal clear,
As PARIAN marble smooth, NARCISSUS hangs

His

His drooping head, and views his image there,
Unhappy flow'r! PANSIES of various hue,
IRIS, and HYACINTH, and ASPHODEL,
To deck the nymph, their richeſt liv'ries wear,
And laviſh all their pride. Nor FLORA's ſelf
More lovely ſmiles, when to the dawning year
Her op'ning boſom heav'nly fragrance breathes.

SEE on yon verdant lawn, the gath'ring crowd
Thicken amain; the buxom nymphs advance
Uſher'd by jolly clowns: diſtinctions ceaſe
Loſt in the common joys, and the bold ſlave
Leans on his wealthy maſter, unreprov'd:
The ſick no pains can feel, no wants the poor.
Round his fond mother's neck the ſmiling babe
Exulting clings; hard by decrepit age
Prop'd on his ſtaff with anxious thought revolves
His pleaſures paſt, and caſts his grave remarks
Among the heedleſs throng. The vig'rous youth
Strips for the combat, hopeful to ſubdue

The fair one's long disdain, by valour now
Glad to convince her coy erroneous heart,
And prove his merit equal to her charms.
Soft pity pleads his cause; blushing she views
His brawny limbs, and his undaunted eye,
That looks a proud defiance on his foes.
Resolv'd, and obstinately firm he stands;
Danger, nor death he fears, while the rich prize
Is victory and love. On the large bough
Of a thick-spreading elm TWANGDILLO sits:
One leg on ISTER's banks the hardy swain
Left undismay'd, BELLONA's light'ning scorch'd
His manly visage, but in pity left
One eye secure. He many a painful bruise
Intrepid felt, and many a gaping wound,
For brown KATE's sake, and for his country's weal:
Yet still the merry bard without regret
Bears his own ills, and with his sounding shell,
And comic phyz, relieves his drooping friends.
Hark, from aloft his tortur'd cat-gut squeals,

He

He tickles ev'ry ſtring, to ev'ry note
He bends his pliant neck, his ſingle eye
Twinkles with joy, his active ſtump beats time,
Let but this ſubtle artiſt ſoftly touch
The trembling chords, the faint expiring ſwain
Trembles no leſs, and the fond yielding maid
Is tweedled into love. See with what pomp
The gaudy bands advance in trim array!
Love beats in ev'ry vein, from ev'ry eye
Darts his contagious flames. They friſk, they bound
Now to the briſk airs, and to the ſpeaking ſtrings:
Attentive, in mid-way the ſexes meet;
Joyous their adverſe fronts they cloſe, and preſs
To ſtrict embrace, as reſolute to force
And ſtorm a paſſage to each other's heart:
Till by the varying notes forewarn'd back they
Recoil diſparted: each with longing eyes
Purſues his mate retiring, till again
The blended ſexes mix; then hand in hand
Faſt lock'd, around they fly, or nimbly wheel

In mazes intricate. The jocund troop,
Pleas'd with their grateful toil, inceſſant ſhake
Their uncouth brawny limbs, and knock their heels
Sonorous; down each brow the trickling balm
In torrents flows, exhaling ſweets refreſh
The gazing croud, and heav'nly fragrance fills
The circuit wide. So danc'd in days of yore,
When ORPHEUS play'd a leſſon to the brutes,
The liſt'ning ſavages; the ſpeckled pard
Dandled the kid, and with the bounding roe
The lion gambol'd. But what heav'nly Muſe
With equal lays ſhall GANDERETTA ſing,
When goddeſs-like ſhe ſkims the verdant plain,
Gracefully gliding? Ev'ry raviſh'd eye
The nymph attracts, and ev'ry heart ſhe wounds,
Thee moſt, tranſported HOBBINOL! Lo, now,
Now to thy op'ning arms ſhe ſkuds along,
With yielding bluſhes glowing on her cheeks;
And eyes that ſweetly languiſh; but too ſoon,
Too ſoon, alas! ſhe flies thy vain embrace,

But

A. Walker del. et Sculp.

But flies to be purſu'd; nimbly ſhe trips,
And darts a glance ſo tender, as ſhe turns,
That with new hopes reliev'd, thy joys revive,
Thy ſtature's rais'd, and thou art more than man.
Thy ſtately port, and more majeſtic air,
And ev'ry ſprightly motion ſpeaks thy love.

To the loud bag-pipe's ſolemn voice attend,
Whoſe riſing winds proclaim a ſtorm is nigh.
Harmonious blaſts! that warm the frozen blood
Of CALEDONIA's ſons to love, or war,
And chear their drooping hearts, robb'd of the ſun's
Enliv'ning ray, that o'er the ſnowy ALPS
Reluctant peeps, and ſpeeds to better climes.

FORTHWITH in hoary majeſty appears
One of gigantic ſize, but viſage wan,
MILONIDES the ſtrong, renown'd of old
For feats of arms, but, bending now with years,
His trunk unwieldy from the verdant turf

He rears deliberate, and with his plant
Of toughest virgin oak in rising aids
His trembling limbs; his bald and wrinkled front,
Entrench'd with many a glorious scar, bespeaks
Submissive rev'rence. He with count'nace grim
Boasts his past deeds, and with redoubled strokes
Marshals the crowd, and forms the circle wide.
Stern arbiter! like some huge rock he stands,
That breaks th' incumbent waves; they throng-
ing press
In troops confus'd, and rear their foaming heads
Each above each, but from superior force
Shrinking repell'd, compose of stateliest view
A liquid theatre. With hands uplift,
And voice STENTORIAN, he proclaims aloud
Each rural prize. "To him whose active foot
"Foils his bold foe, and rivets him to earth,
"This pair of gloves, by curious virgin hands
"Embroider'd, seam'd with silk, and fring'd with
"gold.

"To

"To him, who beſt the ſtubborn hilts can wield,
"And bloody marks of his diſpleaſure leave
"On his opponent's head, this beaver white
"With ſilver edging grac'd, and ſcarlet plume.
"Ye taper maidens! whoſe impetuous ſpeed
"Outflies the roe, nor bends the tender graſs,
"See here this prize, this rich lac'd ſmock behold,
"White as your boſoms, as your kiſſes ſoft.
"Bleſt nymph! whom bounteous Heav'n's pe-
"culiar grace
"Allots this pompous veſt, and worthy deems
"To win a virgin, and to wear a bride."

The gifts refulgent dazzle all the crowd,
In ſpeechleſs admiration fix'd, unmov'd.
Ev'n he who now each glorious palm diſplays,
In ſullen ſilence views his batter'd limbs,
And ſighs his vigour ſpent. Not ſo appall'd
Young Pastorel, for active ſtrength renown'd:
Him Ida bore, a mountain ſhepherdeſs;

On the bleak woald the new-born infant lay,
Expos'd to winter ſnows, and northern blaſts
Severe. As heroes old, who from great JOVE
Derive their proud deſcent, ſo might he boaſt
His line paternal: but be thou, my Muſe!
No leaky blab, nor painful umbrage give
To wealthy 'ſquire, or doughty knight, or peer
Of high degree. Him ev'ry ſhouting ring
In triumph crown'd, him ev'ry champion fear'd,
From * KIFTSGATE to remoteſt * HENBURY.
High in the midſt the brawny wreſtler ſtands,
A ſtately tow'ring object; the tough belt
Meaſures his ample breaſt, and ſhades around
His ſhoulders broad; proudly ſecure he kens
The tempting prize, in his preſumptuous thought
Already gain'd; with partial look the crowd
Approve his claim. But HOBBINOL enrag'd
To ſee th' important gifts ſo cheaply won,

* Two hundreds in GLOCESTERSHIRE.

And uncontested honours tamely lost,
With lowly reverence thus accosts his queen.

"Fair goddess! be propitious to my vows;
"Smile on thy slave, nor Hercules himself
"Shall rob us of this palm: that boaster vain
"Far other port shall learn." She, with a look
That pierc'd his inmost soul, smiling applauds
His gen'rous ardour, with aspiring hope
Distends his breast, and stirs the man within:
Yet much, alas! she fears, for much she loves.
So from her arms the Paphian queen dismiss'd
The warrior god, on glorious slaughter bent,
Provok'd his rage, and with her eyes inflam'd
Her haughty paramour. Swift as the winds
Dispel the fleeting mists, at once he strips
His royal robes; and with a frown that chill'd
The blood of the proud youth, active he bounds
High o'er the heads of multitudes reclin'd:
But as beseem'd one, whose plain honest heart,

Nor passion foul, nor malice dark as Hell,
But honour pure, and love divine had fir'd.
His hand presenting, on his sturdy foe
Disdainfully he smiles; then, quick as thought,
With his left-hand the belt, and with his right
His shoulder seiz'd fast griping; his right-foot
Essay'd the champion's strength, but firm he stood,
Fix'd as a mountain-ash, and in his turn
Repaid the bold affront; his horny fist
Fast on his back he clos'd, and shook in air
The cumb'rous load. Nor rest, nor pause allow'd,
Their watchful eyes instruct their busy feet;
They pant, they heave, each nerve, each sinew's strain'd,
Grasping they close, beneath each painful gripe
The livid tumours rise, in briny streams
The sweat distils, and from their batter'd shins
The clotted gore distains the beaten ground.
Each swain his wish, each trembling nymph conceals

Her

Her ſecret dread; while ev'ry panting breaſt
Alternate fears, and hopes, depreſs or raiſe.
Thus long in dubious ſcale the conteſt hung,
Till PASTOREL impatient of delay,
Collecting all his force, a furious ſtroke
At his left ancle aim'd; 'twas death to fall,
To ſtand impoſſible. O GANGERETTA!
What horrors ſeize thy ſoul! on thy pale cheeks
The roſes fade. But wav'ring long in air,
Nor firm on foot, nor as yet wholly fall'n,
On his right knee he ſlip'd, and nimbly 'ſcap'd
The foul diſgrace. Thus on the ſlacken'd rope
The wingy-footed artiſt, frail ſupport!
Stands tott'ring; now in dreadful ſhrieks the croud
Lament his ſudden fate, and yield him loſt:
He on his hams, or on his brawny rump
Sliding ſecure, derides their vain diſtreſs.
Up ſtarts the vigorous HOBBINOL undiſmay'd,
From mother Earth like old ANTÆUS rais'd
With might redoubled. Clamour and applauſe

Shake all the neighb'ring hills, AVONA's banks
Return him loud acclaim: with ardent eyes,
Fierce as a tyger rufhing from his lair,
He grafp'd the wrift of his infulting foe.
Then with quick wheel oblique his fhoulder point
Beneath his breaft he fix'd, and whirl'd aloft
High o'er his head the fprawling youth he flung:
The hollow ground rebellow'd as he fell.
The crowd prefs forward with tumultuous din;
Thofe to relieve their faint expiring friend,
With gratulations thefe. Hands, tongues, and caps,
Outrageous joy proclaim, fhrill fiddles fqueak,
Hoarfe bag-pipes roar, and GANDERETTA fmiles.

END of the FIRST CANTO.

ARGUMENT of the Second CANTO.

THE *fray.* TONSORIO, COLIN, HILDEBRAND, CUDDY, CINDARAXA, TALGOL, AVARO, CUBBIN, COLLAKIN, MUNDUNGO. *Sir* RHADAMANTH *the justice, attended with his guards, comes to quell the fray.* RHADAMANTH'*s speech. Tumult appeas'd.* GORGONIUS *the butcher takes up the hilts; his character. The* KIFTSGATIANS *consternation, look wistfully on* HOBBINOL; *his speech. The cudgel-playing.* GORGONIUS *knock'd down, falls upon* TWANGDILLO; *his distress; his lamentation over his broken fiddle.*

CANTO II.

LONG while an universal hubbub loud,
Deaf'ning each ear, had drown'd each accent mild;
Till biting taunts, and harsh opprobrious words
Vile utt'rance found. How weak are human minds!
How impotent to stem the swelling tide,
And without insolence enjoy success!
The vale-inhabitants, proud, and elate
With victory, know no restraint, but give
A loose to joy. Their champion HOBBINOL
Vaunting they raise, above that earth-born race
Of giants old, who piling hills on hills,
PELION on OSSA, with rebellious aim
Made war on JOVE. The sturdy mountaineers,

Who

Who ſaw their mightieſt fall'n, and in his fall
Their honours paſt impair'd, their trophies, won
By their proud fathers, who with ſcorn look'd down
Upon the ſubject vale, ſullied, deſpoil'd,
And levell'd with the duſt, no longer bear
The keen reproach. But as when ſudden fire
Seizes the ripen'd grain, whoſe bending ears
Invite the reaper's hand, the furious god
In ſooty triumph rides dreadful, upborn
On wings of wind, that with deſtructive breath
Feed the fierce flames; from ridge to ridge he bounds
Wide-waſting, and pernicious ruin ſpreads:
So thro' the croud from breaſt to breaſt ſwift flew
The propagated rage; loud vollied oaths,
Like thunder burſting from a cloud, gave ſigns
Of wrath awak'd. Prompt fury ſoon ſupplied
With arms uncouth; tough well-ſeaſon'd plants
Weighty with lead infus'd, on either hoſt
Fall thick, and heavy; ſtools in pieces rent,

And chairs, and forms, and batter'd bowls are hurl'd
With fell intent; like bombs the bottles fly
Hiſſing in air, their ſharp-edg'd fragments drench'd
In the warm ſpouting gore; heaps driv'n on heaps
Promiſcuous lie. TONSORIO now advanc'd
On the rough edge of battle: his broad front
Beneath his ſhining helm ſecure, as erſt
Was thine, MAMBRINO, ſtout IBERIAN knight!
Defied the rattling ſtorm, that on his head
Fell innocent. A table's ragged frame
In his right-hand he bore, HERCULEAN club!
Crowds, puſh'd on crowds, before his potent arm
Fled ignominious; havock, and diſmay,
Hung on their rear. COLLIN a merry ſwain,
Blith as the ſoaring lark, as ſweet the ſtrains
Of his ſoft-warbling lips, that whiſtling chear
His lab'ring team, they toſs their heads well pleas'd,
In gaudy plumage deck'd, with ſtern diſdain
Beheld this victor proud; his gen'rous ſoul

Brook'd not the foul diſgrace. High o'er his head
His pond'rous plough-ſtaff in both hands he rais'd;
Erect he ſtood, and ſtretching ev'ry nerve,
As from a forceful engine, down it fell
Upon his hollow'd helm, that yielding ſunk
Beneath the blow, and with its ſharpen'd edge
Shear'd both his ears, they on his ſhoulders broad
Hung ragged. Quick as thought the vig'rous youth
Short'ning his ſtaff, the other end he darts
Into his gaping jaws. Tonsorio fled
Sore maim'd; with pounded teeth and clotted gore
Half-choak'd, he fled; with him the hoſt retir'd,
Companions of his ſhame; all but the ſtout,
And erſt unconquer'd Hildebrand, brave man!
Bold champion of the hill! thy weighty blows
Our fathers felt diſmay'd; to keep thy poſt
Unmov'd, whilom thy valour's choice, now ſad
Neceſſity compels; decrepit now
With age, and ſtiff with honourable wounds,

He

He ſtands unterrify'd: one crutch ſuſtains
His frame majeſtic, th' other in his hand
He wields tremendous; like a mountain boar
In toils inclos'd, he dares his circling foes.
They ſhrink aloof, or ſoon with ſhame repent
The raſh aſſault, the ruſtic heroes fall
In heaps around. CUDDY, a dextrous youth,
When force was vain, on fraudful art rely'd:
Cloſe to the ground low-cow'ring, unperceiv'd,
Cautious he crept, and with his crooked bill
Cut ſheer the frail ſupport, prop of his age:
Reeling a while he ſtood, and menac'd fierce
Th' inſidious ſwain, reluctant now at length
Fell prone and plough'd the duſt. So the tall oak,
Old monarch of the groves, that long had ſtood
The ſhock of warring winds, and the red bolts
Of angry JOVE, ſhorn of his leafy ſhade
At laſt, and inwardly decay'd, if chance
The cruel woodman ſpy the friendly ſpur,

His

His only hold; that sever'd, soon he nods,
And shakes th' incumber'd mountain as he falls.

WHEN manly-valour fail'd, a female arm
Restor'd the fight. As in th' adjacent booth
Black CINDARAXA's busy hand prepar'd
The smoaky viands, she beheld, abash'd,
The routed host, and all her dastard friends
Far scattered o'er the plain; their shameful flight
Griev'd her proud heart, for hurry'd with the stream
Ev'n TALGOL too had fled, her darling boy.
A flaming brand from off the glowing hearth
The greasy heroine snatch'd; o'er her pale foes
The threat'ning meteor shone, brandish'd in air,
Or round their heads in ruddy circles play'd.
Across the prostrate HILDEBRAND she strode,
Dreadfully bright: the multitude appall'd
Fled diff'rent ways, their beards, their hair in flames.

Imprudent ſhe purſu'd, till on the brink
Of the next pool, with force united preſs'd,
And waving round with huge two-handed ſway
Her blazing arms, into the muddy lake
The bold virago fell. Dire was the fray
Between the warring elements; of old
Thus MULCIBER, and XANTHUS DARDAN ſtream
In hideous battle join'd. Juſt ſinking now
Into the boiling deep, with ſuppliant hands
She begg'd for life; black ouſe and filth obſcene
Hung in her matted hair; the ſhouting croud
Inſult her woes, and proud of their ſucceſs,
The dripping Amazon in triumph lead.
Now, like a gath'ring ſtorm, the rally'd troops
Blacken'd the plain. Young TALGOL from their front,
With a fond lover's haſte, ſwift as the hind,
That, by the huntſman's voice alarm'd, had fled
Panting returns, and ſeeks the gloomy brake,

Where

Where her dear fawn lay hid, into the booth
Impatient rufh'd. But when the fatal tale
He heard, the dearest treafure of his foul
Purloin'd, his CINDY loft; ftiff'ned and pale
A while he ftood; his kindling ire at length
Burft forth implacable, and injur'd love
Shot light'ning from his eyes; a fpit he feiz'd,
Juft reeking from the fat furloin, a long,
Unwieldy fpear; then with impetuous rage
Prefs'd forward on th' embattled hoft, that fhrunk
At his approach. The rich AVARO firft,
His flefhy rump bor'd with difhoneft wounds,
Fled bellowing; nor could his num'rous flocks,
Nor all th' afpiring pyramids that grace
His yard well ftor'd, fave the penurious clown.
Here CUBBIN fell, and there young COLLAKIN,
Nor his fond mother's pray'rs nor ardent vows
Of love-fick maids could move relentlefs Fate.
Where'er he rag'd, with his far-beaming lance

He thinn'd their ranks, and all their battle ſwerv'd.
With many an inroad gor'd. Then caſt around
His furious eyes, if haply he might find
The captive fair; her in the duſt he ſpy'd
Grov'ling, diſconſolate; thoſe locks, that erſt,
So bright, ſhone like the poliſh'd jet, defil'd
With mire impure; thither with eager haſte
He ran, he flew. But when the wretched maid
Proſtrate he view'd, deform'd with gaping wounds
And welt'ring in her blood, his trembling hand
Soon drop'd the dreaded lance; on her pale cheeks
Ghaſtly he gaz'd, nor felt the pealing ſtorm,
That on his bare defenceleſs brow fell thick
From ev'ry arm: o'erpower'd at laſt, down ſunk
His drooping head, on her cold breaſt reclin'd.
Hail, faithful pair! if ought my verſe avail,
Nor Envy's ſpite, nor time ſhall e'er efface
The records of your fame; blind BRITISH bards
In ages yet to come, on feſtal days

Shall

Shall chant this mournful tale, while liſt'ning nymphs
Lament around, and ev'ry gen'rous heart
With active valour glows, and virtuous love.
How blind is pop'lar fury ! how perverſe,
When broils inteſtine rage, and force controuls
Reaſon and law ! As the torn veſſel ſinks
Between the burſt of adverſe waves o'erwhelm'd ;
So fares it with the neutral head, between
Contending parties bruis'd, inceſſant peal'd
With random ſtrokes that undiſcerning fall ;
Guiltleſs he ſuffers moſt, who leaſt offends.
MUNDUNGO from the bloody field retir'd,
Cloſe in a corner plied the peaceful bowl ;
Incurious he, and thoughtleſs of events,
Now deem'd himſelf conceal'd, wrapt in the cloud
That iſſu'd from his mouth, and the thick fogs
That hung upon his brows ; but hoſtile rage
Inquiſitive found out the ruſty ſwain.

His ſhort black tube down his furr'd throat impell'd,
Stagg'ring he reel'd, and with tenacious gripe
The bulky jordan, that before him ſtood,
Seiz'd falling; that its liquid freight diſgorg'd
Upon the proſtrate clown; flound'ring he lay
Beneath the muddy bev'rage whelm'd, ſo late
His prime delight. Thus the luxurious waſp,
Voracious inſect, by the fragrant dregs
Allur'd, and in the viſcous nectar plung'd,
His filmy pennons ſtruggling flaps in vain,
Loſt in a flood of ſweets. Still o'er the plain
Fierce onſet, and tumultuous battle ſpread;
And now they fall, and now they riſe, incens'd
With animated rage, while nought around
Is heard, but clamour, ſhout, and female cries,
And curſes mix'd with groans. Diſcord on high
Shook her infernal ſcourge, and o'er their heads
Scream'd with malignant joy; when lo! between
The warring hoſts appear'd ſage RHADAMANTH,

A knight of high renown. Nor QUIXOTE bold,
Nor AMADIS of GAUL, nor HUDIBRAS,
Mirror of knighthood, e'er could vie with thee,
Great ſultan of the vale! thy front ſevere,
As humble INDIANS to their pagods bow,
The clowns ſubmiſs approach. THEMIS to thee
Commits her golden balance, where ſhe weighs
Th' abandon'd orphan's ſighs, the widow's tears;
By thee gives ſure redreſs, comforts the heart
Oppreſs'd with woe, and rears the ſuppliant knee.
Each bold offender hides his guilty head,
Aſtoniſh'd, when thy delegated arm
Draws her vindictive ſword; at thy command,
Stern miniſter of power ſupreme! each ward
Sends forth her brawny myrmidons, their clubs
Blazon'd with royal arms; diſpatchful haſte
Sits earneſt on each brow, and publick care.
Encompaſs'd round with theſe his dreadful guards,
He ſpurr'd his ſober ſteed, grizzled with age,

And venerably dull; his ſtirrups ſtretch'd
Beneath the knightly load; one hand he fix'd
Upon his ſaddle-bow, the other palm
Before him ſpread, like ſome grave orator
In ATHENS, or free ROME, when eloquence
Subdu'd mankind, and all the liſt'ning crowd
Hung by their ears on his perſuaſive tongue.
He thus the jarring multitude addreſs'd.

"NEIGHBOURS, and friends, and countrymen,
"the flow'r
"Of KIFTSGATE! ah! what means this impious
"broil?
"Is then the haughty GAUL no more your care?
"Are LANDEN'S plains ſo ſoon forgot, that thus
"Ye ſpill that blood inglorious, waſte that ſtrength,
"Which, well employ'd, once more might have
"compell'd
"The ſtripling ANJOU to a ſhameful flight?

"Or

" Or by your great forefathers taught, have fix'd
" The BRITISH ſtandard on LUTETIAN tow'rs?
" O ſight odious, deteſtable! O times
" Degenerate, of ancient honour void!
" This fact ſo foul, ſo riotous, inſults
" All law, all ſov'reign pow'r, and calls aloud
" For vengeance; but, my friends! too well ye
" know,
" How ſlow this arm to puniſh, and how bleeds
" This heart, when forc'd on rigorous extremes.
" O countrymen! all, all, can teſtify
" My vigilance, my care for publick good.
" I am the man, who by your own free choice
" Select from all the tribes, in ſenates rul'd
" Each warm debate, and emptied all my ſtores
" Of ancient ſcience in my country's cauſe.
" Wiſe TACITUS, of penetration deep,
" Each ſecret ſpring reveal'd, THUANUS bold
" Breath'd liberty, and all the mighty dead,

" Rais'd at my call, the BRITISH rights confirm'd;
" While MUSGRAVE, HOW, and SEYMOUR
" fneer'd in vain.
" I am the man, who from the bench exalt
" This voice, ftill grateful to your ears, this voice
" Which breathes for you alone. Where is the
" wretch
" Diftrefs'd, who in the cobwebs of the law
" Entangled, and in fubtile problems loft,
" Seeks not to me for aid! In fhoals they come
" Neglected, feelefs clients, nor return
" Unedify'd; fcarce greater multitudes
" At DELPHI fought the god, to learn their fate
" From his dark oracles. I am the man,
" Whofe watchful providence beyond the date
" Of this frail life extends, to future times
" Beneficent; my ufeful fchemes fhall fteer
" The common-weal in ages yet to come.
" Your children's children, taught by me, fhall keep

" Their

"Their rights inviolable: and as ROME
"The Sibyl's ſacred books, tho' wrote on leaves
"And ſcatter'd o'er the ground, with pious awe
"Collected; ſo your ſons ſhall glean with care
"My hallow'd fragments, ev'ry ſcrip divine
"Conſult intent, of more intrinſic worth
"Than half a VATICAN. Hear me, my friends!
"Hear me, my countrymen! Oh ſuffer not
"This hoary head, employ'd for you alone,
"To ſink with ſorrow to the grave." He ſpake,
And veil'd his bonnet to the crowd. As when
The ſov'reign of the floods o'er the rough deep
His awful trident ſhakes, its fury falls,
The warring billows on each hand retire,
And foam, and rage no more. All now is huſh'd,
The multitude appeas'd; a chearful dawn
Smiles on the fields, the waving throng ſubſides,
And the loud tempeſt ſinks, becalm'd in peace.

GORGONIUS now with haughty ſtrides advanc'd,
A gauntlet ſeiz'd, firm on his guard he ſtood
A formidable foe, and dealt in air
His empty blows, a prelude to the fight.
Slaughter his trade; full many a pamper'd ox
Fell by his fatal hand, the bulky beaſt
Dragg'd by his horns, oft at one deadly blow,
His iron fiſt deſcending cruſh'd his ſkull,
And left him ſpurning on the bloody floor,
While at his feet the guiltleſs axe was laid.
In dubious fight of late one eye he loſt,
Bor'd from its orb, and the next glancing ſtroke
Bruis'd ſore the riſing arch, and bent his noſe:
Nathleſs he triumph'd on the well-fought ſtage,
HOCKLEIAN hero! Nor was more deform'd
The CYCLOPS blind, nor of more monſtrous ſize,
Nor his void orb more dreadful to behold,
Weeping the putrid gore, ſevere revenge
Of ſubtile ITHACUS. Terribly gay

In

In his buff doublet, larded o'er with fat
Of ſlaughter'd brutes, the well-oil'd champion
ſhone.
Sternly he gaz'd around, with many a frown
Fierce menacing, provok'd the tardy foe.
For now each combatant, that erſt ſo bold
Vaunted his manly deeds, in penſive mood
Hung down his head, and fix'd on earth his eyes,
Pale and diſmay'd. On HOBBINOL at laſt
Intent they gaze, in him alone their hope,
Each eye ſollicits him, each panting heart
Joins in the ſilent ſuit. Soon he perceiv'd
Their ſecret wiſh, and eas'd their doubting minds.

"YE men of KIFTSGATE! whoſe wide ſpread-
"ing fame
"In antient days were ſung from ſhore to ſhore,
"To BRITISH bards of old a copious theme;
"Too well, alas! in your pale cheeks I view
"Your

"Your daſtard ſouls. O mean, degen'rate race!
"But ſince on me ye call, each ſuppliant eye
"Invites my ſov'reign aid, lo! here I come,
"The bulwark of your fame, tho' ſcarce my brows
"Are dry from glorious toils, juſt now atchiev'd,
"To vindicate your worth. Lo! here I ſwear,
"By all my great forefathers fair renown,
"By that illuſtrious wicker, where they ſat
"In comely pride, and in triumphant ſloth
"Gave law to paſſive clowns; or on this ſpot
"In glory's prime, young HOBBINOL expires,
"And from his deareſt GANDERETTA's arms
"Sink's to Death's cold embrace; or by this hand
"That ſtranger, big with inſolence, ſhall fall
"Prone on the ground, and do your honour
"right."

FORTHWITH the hilts he ſeiz'd; but on his arm
Fond GANDERETTA hung, and round his neck

A. Walker del. et Sculp.

Curl'd in a ſoft embrace. Honour and love
A doubtful conteſt wag'd, but from her ſoon
He ſprung relentleſs, all her tears were vain,
Yet oft he turn'd, oft ſigh'd, thus pleading mild:

"Ill ſhould I merit theſe imperial robes,
"Enſigns of majeſty, by gen'ral voice
"Conferr'd, ſhould pain, or death itſelf avail
"To ſhake the ſteady purpoſe of my ſoul.
"Peace, fair one! Heaven will protect the man,
"By thee held dear, and crown thy gen'rous love."

Her from the liſted field the matrons ſage
Reluctant drew, and with fair ſpeeches ſooth'd.

Now front to front the fearleſs champions meet;
Gorgonius like a tow'r, whoſe cloudy top
Invades the ſkies, ſtood low'ring; far beneath
The ſtripling Hobbinol with careful eye

Each op'ning ſcans, and each unguarded ſpace
Meaſures intent. While negligently bold,
The bulky combatant, whoſe heart elate
Diſdain'd his puny foe, now fondly deem'd
At one deciſive ſtroke to win, unhurt,
An eaſy victory; down came at once
The pond'rous plant, with fell malicious rage,
Aim'd at his head direct; but the tough hilts,
Swift interpos'd, elude his effort vain.
The cautious HOBBINOL, with ready feet,
Now ſhifts his ground, retreating; then again
Advances bold and his unguarded ſhins
Batters ſecure; each well-directed blow
Bites to the quick; thick as the falling hail,
The ſtrokes redoubled peal his hollow ſides:
The multitude amaz'd with horror view
The rattling ſtorm, ſhrink back at ev'ry blow,
And ſeem to feel his wounds; inly he groan'd,
And gnaſh'd his teeth, and from his blood-ſhot eye

Red

Red lightning flaſh'd the fierce tumultuous rage
Shook all his mighty fabric; once again
Erect he ſtands, collected, and reſolv'd
To conquer, or to die: ſwift as the bolt
Of angry JOVE, the weighty plant deſcends.
But wary HOBBINOL, whoſe watchful eye
Perceiv'd his kind intent, ſlip'd on one ſide
Declining; the vain ſtroke from ſuch an height,
With ſuch a force impell'd, headlong drew down
Th' unwieldy champion: on the ſolid ground
He fell rebounding breathleſs, and aſtunn'd,
His trunk extended lay; ſore maim'd from out
His heaving breaſt, he belch'd a crimſon flood.
Full leiſurely he roſe, but conſcious ſhame
Of honour loſt his failing ſtrength renew'd.
Rage, and revenge, and ever-during hate,
Blacken'd his ſtormy front; raſh, furious, blind,
And laviſh of his blood, of random ſtrokes
He laid on load; without deſign or art!

N Onward

Onward he preſs'd outrageous, while his foes
Encircling wheels, or inch by inch retires,
Wiſe niggard of his ſtrength. Yet all thy care,
O HOBBINOL! avail'd not to prevent
One hapleſs blow; o'er his ſtrong guard the plant
Lapp'd pliant, and its knotty point impreſs'd
His nervous chine; he wreath'd him to and fro
Convolv'd, yet thus diſtreſs'd, intrepid bore
His hilts aloft, and guarded well his head.
So when the unwary clown, with haſty ſtep,
Cruſhes the folded ſnake, her wounded parts
Grov'ling ſhe trails along, but her high creſt
Erect ſhe bears; in all its ſpeckled pride,
She ſwells inflam'd, and with her forky tongue
Threatens deſtruction. With like eager haſte,
Th' impatient HOBBINOL, whoſe exceſſive pain
Stung to his heart, a ſpeedy vengeance vow'd,
Nor wanted long the means; a feint he made
With well-diſſembled guile, his batter'd ſhins

Mark'd with his eyes, and menac'd with his plant.
Gorgonius, whose long-suff'ring legs scarce bore
His cumb'rous bulk; to his supporters frail
Indulgent, soon the friendly hilts oppos'd;
Betray'd, deceiv'd, on his unguarded crest
The stroke delusive fell; a dismal groan
Burst from his hollow chest; his trembling hands
Forsook the hilts, across the spacious ring
Backward he reel'd, the crowd affrighted fly
T' escape the falling ruin. But, alas!
'Twas thy hard fate, Twangdillo! to receive
His pond'rous trunk; on thee, on helpless thee,
Headlong, and heavy, the foul monster fell.
Beneath a mountain's weight, th' unhappy bard
Lay prostrate, nor was more renown'd thy song,
O seer of Thrace! nor more severe thy fate.
His vocal shell, the solace and support
Of wretched age, gave one melodious scream,
And in a thousand fragemnts strew'd the plain.

The nymphs, ſure friends to his harmonious mirth,
Fly to his aid, his hairy breaſt expoſe
To each refreſhing gale, and with ſoft hands
His temples chafe; at their perſuaſive touch
His fleeting ſoul returns; upon his rump
He ſat diſconſolate; but when, alas!
He view'd the ſhatter'd fragments, down again
He ſunk expiring; by their friendly care
Once more reviv'd, he thrice aſſay'd to ſpeak,
And thrice the riſing ſobs his voice ſubdu'd:
Till thus at laſt his wretched plight he mourn'd.

" SWEET inſtrument of mirth! ſole comfort left
" To my declining years! whoſe ſprightly notes
" Reſtor'd my vigour, and renew'd my bloom,
" Soft healing balm to ev'ry wounded heart!
" Deſpairing, dying ſwains, from the cold ground
" Uprais'd by thee, at thy melodious call,
" With raviſh'd ears receiv'd the flowing joy.

" Gay

" Gay pleaſantry, and care-beguiling joke,
" Thy ſure attendants were, and at thy voice
" All nature ſmil'd. But, oh this hand no more
" Shall touch thy wanton ſtrings, no more with lays
" Alternate, from oblivion dark redeem
" The mighty dead, and vindicate their fame.
" Vain are thy toils, O HOBBINOL! and all
" Thy triumphs vain. Who ſhall record, brave man!
" Thy bold exploits? Who ſhall thy grandeur tell,
" Supreme of KIFTSGATE? See thy faithful bard,
" Deſpoil'd, undone. O cover me, ye hills!
" Whoſe vocal clifts were taught my joyous ſong.
" Or thou, fair nymph, AVONA, on whoſe banks
" The frolick crowd, led by my num'rous ſtrains,
" Their orgies keep'd, and friſk'd it o'er the green,
" Jocund, and gay, while thy remurm'ring ſtreams
" Danc'd by, well pleas'd. Oh! let thy friendly
" waves
" O'erwhelm a wretch, and hide this head ac-
" curs'd."

So plains the reſtleſs PHILOMEL, her neſt,
And callow young, the tender growing hope,
Of future harmony, and frail return
For all her cares, to barb'rous churls a prey;
Darkling ſhe ſings, the woods repeat her moan.

End of the SECOND CANTO.

ARGUMENT of the Third CANTO.

GOOD *eating expedient for heroes.* HOMER *praised for keeping a table.* HOBBINOL *triumphant.* GANDERETTA's *bill of fare. Panegyrick upon ale. Gossipping over a bottle. Compliment to Mr.* JOHN PHILLIPS. GANDERETTA's *perplexity discovered by* HOBBINOL; *his consolatory speech; compares himself to* GUY *Earl of* WARWICK. GANDERETTA *encouraged, strips for the race; her amiable figure.* FUSCA *the gypsy, her dirty figure.* TABITHA *her great reputation for speed; hired to the dissenting academy at* TEWKSBURY. *A short account of* GAMALIEL *the master, and his hopeful scholars.* TABITHA *carries weight. The smock race.* TABITHA's *fall.* FUSCA's *short triumph, her humiliation.* GANDERETTA's *matchless speed.* HOBBINOL *lays the prize at her feet. Their mutual triumph. The vicissitude of human affairs, experienced by* HOBBINOL. MOPSA, *formerly his servant, with her two children apperas to him.* MOPSA's *speech; assaults* GANDERETTA; *her flight.* HOBBINOL's *prodigious fright; is taken into custody by constables, and dragged to Sir* RHADAMANTH's.

CANTO III.

THO' some of old, and some of modern date,
Penurious their victorious heroes fed
With barren praise alone; yet thou, my Muse!
Benevolent, with more indulgent eyes
Behold th' immortal HOBBINOL; reward
With due regalement his triumphant toils.
Let QUIXOTE's hardy courage, and renown,
With SANCHO's prudent care be meetly join'd.

O THOU of bards supreme, MÆONIDES!
What well-fed heroes grace thy hallow'd page!
Laden with glorious spoils, and gay with blood
Of slaughter'd hosts, the victor chief returns.
Whole TROY before him fled, and men, and gods,

Oppos'd in vain. For the brave man, whoſe arm
Repell'd his country's wrong, ev'n he, the great
Atrides, king of kings, even he prepares
With his own royal hand the ſumptuous feaſt.
Full to the brim, the brazen cauldrons ſmoke,
Thro' all the buſy camp the riſing blaze
Atteſt their joy; heroes, and kings forego
Their ſtate, and pride, and at his elbow wait
Obſequious. On a poliſh'd charger plac'd,
The bulky chine with plenteous fat inlaid,
Of golden hue, magnificently ſhines.
The choiceſt morſels ſever'd to the gods,
The hero next, well paid for all his wounds,
The rich repaſt divides with Jove; from out
The ſparkling bowl he draws the gen'rous wine,
Unmix'd, unmeaſur'd; with unſtinted joy
His heart o'erflows. In like triumphant port
Sat the victorious Hobbinol; the crowd
Tranſported view, and bleſs their glorious chief:

All

All KIFTSGATE ſounds his praiſe with joint ac-
claim.
Him ev'ry voice, him ev'ry knee confeſs,
In merit, as in right, their king. Upon
The flow'ry turf, Earth's painted lap, are ſpread
The rural dainties; ſuch as Nature boon
Preſents with laviſh hand, or ſuch as owe
To GANDERETTA's care their grateful taſte,
Delicious. For ſhe long ſince prepar'd
To celebrate this day, and with good chear
To grace his triumphs. Cryſtal gooſeberries
Are pil'd on heaps; in vain the parent tree
Defends her luſcious fruit with pointed ſpears.
The ruby-tinctur'd corinth cluſt'ring hangs,
And emulates the grape; green codlings float
In dulcet creams; nor wants the laſt year's ſtore,
The hardy nut, in ſolid mail ſecure,
Impregnable to winter froſts, repays
Its hoarder's care. The cuſtard's gellied flood

Impatient

Impatient youth, with greedy joy, devours.
Cheesecakes and pies, in various forms uprais'd,
In well-built pyramids, aspiring stand.
Black hams, and tongues, that speechless can persuade
To ply the brisk carouse, and chear the soul
With jovial draughts. Nor does the jolly god
Deny his precious gifts; here jocund swains,
In uncouth mirth delighted, sporting quaff
Their native bev'rage; in the brimming glass
The liquid amber smiles. BRITONS, no more
Dread your invading foes; let the false GAUL,
Of rule insatiate, potent to deceive,
And great by subtile wiles, from th' adverse shore
Pour forth his num'rous hosts; IBERIA! join
Thy tow'ring fleets, once more aloft display
Thy consecrated banners, fill thy sails
With pray'rs and vows, most formidably strong
In holy trump'ry, let old Ocean groan

Beneath

Beneath the proud ARMADA vainly deem'd
Invincible; yet fruitless all their toils,
Vain ev'ry rash effort, while our fat glebe,
Of barley-grain productive, still supplies
The flowing treasure, and with sums immense
Supports the throne; while this rich cordial warms
The farmer's courage, arms his stubborn soul
With native honour, and resistless rage.
Thus vaunt the crowd, each freeborn heart o'er-
flows
With BRITAIN's glory, and his country's love.

HERE, in a merry knot combin'd, the nymphs
Pour out mellifluous streams, the balmy spoils
Of the laborious bee. The modest maid
But coyly sips, and blushing drinks, abash'd:
Each lover with observant eye beholds
Her graceful shame, and at her glowing cheeks
Rekindles all his fires, but matrons sage,

Better

Better experienc'd, and inſtructed well
In midnight myſteries, and feaſt-rites old,
Graſp the capacious bowl; nor ceaſe to draw
The ſpumy nectar. Healths of gay import
Fly merrily about; now Scandal ſly
Inſinuating gilds the ſpecious tale
With treach'rous praiſe, and with a double face
Ambiguous Wantonneſs demurely ſneers:
Till circling brimmers ev'ry veil withdraw,
And dauntleſs Impudence appears unmaſk'd.
Others apart, in the cool ſhade retir'd,
SILURIAN cyder quaff, by that great bard
Ennobled, who firſt taught my grov'ling Muſe
To mount aerial. O! could I but raiſe
My feeble voice to his exalted ſtrains,
Or to the height of this great argument,
The gen'rous liquid in each line ſhou'd bound
Spirit'ous, nor oppreſſive cork ſubdue
Its foaming rage; but to the lofty theme
Unequal, Muſe, decline the pleaſing taſk.

THUS

THUS they luxurious, on the grassy turf,
Revell'd at large: while nought around was heard
But mirth confus'd, and undistinguish'd joy,
And laughter far resounding; serious Care
Found here no place; to GANDERETTA's breast
Retiring; there with hopes, and fears perplex'd
Her fluctuating mind. Hence the soft sigh
Escapes unheeded, spight of all her art;
The trembling blushes on her lovely cheeks,
Alternate ebb, and flow; from the full glass
She flies abstemious, shuns th' untasted feast:
But careful HOBBINOL, whose am'rous eye
From hers ne'er wander'd, haunting still the place
Where his dear treasure lay, discover'd soon
Her secret woe, and bore a lover's part.
Compassion melts his soul, her glowing cheeks
He kiss'd, enamour'd, and her panting heart
He press'd to his; then with these soothing words,
Tenderly smiling, her faint hopes reviv'd.

"COURAGE

" Courage, my Fair! the ſplendid prize is
" thine.
" Indulgent Fortune will not damp our joys,
" Nor blaſt the glories of this happy day.
" Hear me, ye ſwains! Ye men of Kiftsgate!
" hear:
" Tho' great the honours by your hands conferr'd,
" Theſe royal ornaments, tho' great the force
" Of this puiſſant arm, as all muſt own,
" Who ſaw this day the bold Gorgonius fall;
" Yet were I more renown'd for feats of arms,
" And knightly prowefs, than that mighty Guy,
" So fam'd in antique ſong, Warwick's great earl
" Who ſlew the gaint Colbrand, in fierce fight
" Maintain'd a ſummer's day, and freed this realm
" From Danish vaſſalage; his pond'rous ſword,
" And maſſy ſpear, atteſt the glorious deed;
" Nor leſs his hoſpitable ſoul is ſeen
" In that capacious cauldron, whoſe large freight

" Might

"Might feaſt a province; yet were I like him
"The nation's pride, like him I cou'd forego
"All earthly grandeur, wander thro' the world:
"A jocund pilgrim, in the loneſome den,
"And rocky cave, with theſe my royal hands
"Scoop the cold ſtreams, with herbs, and roots
"content,
"Mean ſuſtenance; could I by this but gain
"For the dear Fair, the prize her heart deſires.
"Believe me, charming maid! I'd be a worm,
"The meaneſt inſect, and the loweſt thing
"The world deſpiſes, to enhance thy fame."
So chear'd he his fair queen, and ſhe was chear'd.

Now with a noble confidence inſpir'd,
Her looks aſſure ſucceſs, now ſtripp'd of all
Her cumb'rous veſtments, beauty's vain diſguiſe,
She ſhines unclouded in her native charms.
Her plaited hair behind her in a brede
Hung

Hung careless, with becoming grace each blush
Varied her cheeks, than the gay rising dawn
More lovely, when the new-born light salutes
The joyful Earth, impurpling half the skies.
Her heaving breast, thro' the thin cov'ring view'd,
Fix'd each beholder's eye; her taper thighs,
And lineaments exact, wou'd mock the skill
Of PHIDIAS; Nature alone can form
Such due proportion. To compare with her
OREAD, or DRYAD, or of DELIA's train,
Fair virgin huntress, for the chace array'd
With painted quiver, and unerring bow,
Were but to lessen her superior mien,
And goddess-like deport. The master's hand,
Rare artisan! with proper shades improves
His lively colouring; so here, to grace
Her brighter charms, next her upon the plain
FUSCA the brown appears, with greedy eye
Views the rich prize, her tawny front erects

Audacious, and with her legs unclean;
Booted with grim, and with her freckled ſkin
Offends the crowd. She of the Gypſy train
Had wander'd long, and the ſun's ſcorching rays
Imbrown'd her viſage grim; artful to view
The ſpreading palm, and with vile cant deceive
The love-ſick maid, who barters all her ſtore
For airy viſions and fallacious hope.
GORGONIUS, if the current fame ſay true,
Her comrade once, they many a merry prank
Together play'd, and many a mile had ſtroll'd,
For him fit mate. Next TABITHA the tall
Strode o'er the plain, with huge gigantick pace,
And overlook'd the crowd, known far and near
For matchleſs ſpeed; ſhe many a prize had won,
Pride of that neighb'ring * mart, for muſtard fam'd,
Sharp-biting grain, where amicably join

* TEWKSBURY in the Vale of EVESHAM, where the AVON runs into the SEVERN.

The ſiſter floods, and with their liquid arms
Greeting embrace. Here GAMALIEL ſage,
Of CAMERONIAN brood, with ruling rod
Trains up his babes of grace, inſtructed well
In all the gainful diſcipline of pray'r,
To point the holy leer, by juſt degrees
To cloſe the twinkling eye, t' expand the palms,
T' expoſe the whites, and with the ſightleſs ball
To glare upon the crowd, to raiſe, or ſink
The docile voice, now murm'ring ſoft and low
With inward accent calm, and then again
In foaming floods of rapt'rous eloquence,
Let looſe the ſtorm, and thunder thro' the noſe
The threat'ned vengeance: ev'ry muſe profane
Is baniſh'd hence, and HELICONIAN ſtreams
Deſerted, the fam'd LEMAN lake ſupplies
More plenteous draughts, of more divine import.
Hail, happy youths! on whom indulgent Heav'n
Each grace divine beſtows, nor yet denies

Carnal beatitudes, ſweet privilege
Of ſaints elect! Royal prerogative!
Here in domeſtick cares employ'd and bound
To annual ſervitude, frail TABITHA
Her priſtine vigour loſt, now mourns in vain
Her ſharpen'd viſage, and the ſickly qualms
That grieve her ſoul; a prey to Love, while Grace
Slept heedleſs by: yet her undaunted mind
Still meditates the prize, and ſtill ſhe hopes,
Beneath th' unwieldy load, her wonted ſpeed.
Others of meaner fame the ſtately Muſe
Records not; on more lofty flights intent
She ſpurns the ground, and mounts her native ſkies.

ROOM for the maſter of the ring; ye ſwains!
Divide your crowded ranks. See! there on high
The glitt'ring prize, on the tall ſtandard born,
Waving in air; before him march in files
The rural minſtrelſy, the rattling drum

A. Walker del. et Sculp.

[illegible]

[illegible]

[illegible]

[illegible]

[illegible]

[illegible]

[illegible]

[illegible]

[illegible]

[illegible]

[illegible]

[illegible]

[illegible]

[illegible]

Of ſolemn ſound, and th' animating horn,
Each huntſman's joy; the tabor and the pipe,
Companion dear at feaſts, whoſe chearful notes
Give life, and motion to th' unwieldy clown.
Ev'n Age revives; and the pale puking maid
Feels ruddy health rekindling on her cheeks,
And with new vigour trips it o'er the plain.
Counting each careful ſtep, he paces o'er
Th' allotted ground, and fixes at the goal
His ſtandard, there himſelf majeſtic ſwells.
Stretch'd in a line, the panting rivals wait
Th' expected ſignal, with impatient eyes
Meaſure the ſpace between, and in conceit
Already graſp the warm-conteſted prize.
Now all at once ruſh forward to the goal,
And ſtep by ſtep, and ſide by ſide, they ply
Their buſy feet, and leave the crowd behind.
Quick heaves each breaſt, and quick they ſhoot along,

Thro' the divided air, and bound it o'er the plain.
To this, to that, capricious Fortune deals
Short hopes, ſhort fears, and momentary joy.
The breathleſs throng with open throats purſue,
And broken accents ſhout imperfect praiſe.
Such noiſe confus'd is heard, ſuch wild uproar,
When on the main the ſwelling ſurges riſe,
Daſh o'er the rocks, and hurrying thro' the flood,
Drive on each others backs, and crowd the ſtrand.
Before the reſt tall TABITHA was ſeen,
Stretching amain, and whirling o'er the field;
Swift as the ſhooting ſtar that gilds the night
With rapid tranſient blaze, ſhe runs, ſhe flies;
Sudden ſhe ſtops, nor longer can endure
The painful courſe, but drooping ſinks away,
And like that falling meteor, there ſhe lies
A jelly cold on earth. FUSCA, with joy,
Beheld her wretched plight; o'er the pale corſe
Inſulting bounds; Hope gave her wings, and now

Exerting

Exerting all her ſpeed, ſtep after ſtep,
At GANDERETTA's elbow urg'd her way,
Her ſhoulder preſſing, and with pois'nous breath
Tainting her iv'ry neck. Long while had held
The ſharp conteſt, had not propitious Heav'n,
With partial hands, to ſuch tranſcendent charms
Diſpens'd its favours. For as o'er the green
The careleſs Gypſy, with incautious ſpeed,
Puſh'd forward, and her rival Fair had reach'd
With equal pace, and only not o'erpaſs'd:
Haply ſhe treads, where late the merry train,
In waſteful luxury, and wanton joy,
Laviſh had ſpilt the cyder's frothy flood,
And mead with cuſtard mix'd. Surpriz'd, appall'd,
And in the treach'rous puddle ſtruggling long,
She ſlipp'd, ſhe fell, upon her back ſupine
Extended lay; the laughing multitude
With noiſy ſcorn approv'd her juſt diſgrace.
As the ſleek lev'ret ſkims before the pack,

So flies the nymph, and so the crowd pursue.
Born on the wings of wind the Dear One flies,
Swift as the various goddess, nor less bright
In beauty's prime, when thro' the yielding air
She darts along, and with refracted rays
Paints the gay clouds; celestial messenger,
Charg'd with the high behests of Heav'n's great queen!
Her at the goal with open arms receiv'd
Fond HOBBINOL; with active leap he seiz'd
The costly prize, and laid it at her feet.
Then pausing stood, dumb with excess of joy,
Expressive silence! for each tender glance
Betray'd the raptures that his tongue conceal'd.
Less mute the crowd, in echoing shouts, applaud
Her speed, her beauty, his obsequious love.

UPON a little eminence, whose top
O'er look'd the plain, a steep, but short ascent,

Plac'd

Plac'd in a chair of state, with garlands crown'd,
And loaded with the fragrance of the spring,
Fair GANDERETTA shone; like mother EVE
In her gay sylvan lodge, delicious bow'r!
Where Nature's wanton hand, above the reach
Of rule, or art, had lavish'd all her store,
To deck the flow'ry roof; and at her side,
Imperial HOBBINOL, with front sublime
Great as a ROMAN consul, just return'd
From cities sack'd, and provinces laid waste,
In his paternal wicker sat, enthron'd.
With eager eyes the crowd about them press,
Ambitious to behold the happy pair.
Each voice, each instrument, proclaims their joy
With loudest vehemence: such noise is heard,
Such a tumultuous din, when at the call
Of BRITAIN's sovereign, the rustick bands
O'erspread the fields; the subtile candidates
Dissembled homage pay, and court the fools

Whom they despise; each proud majestic clown
Looks big, and shouts amain, mad with the taste
Of pow'r supreme, frail empire of a day!
That with the setting sun extinct is lost.

Nor is thy grandeur, mighty Hobbinol!
Of longer date. Short is, alas! the reign
Of mortal pride: we play our parts a while,
And strut upon the stage; the scene is chang'd,
And offers us a dungeon for a throne.
Wretched vicissitude! for after all
His tinsel dreams of empire and renown,
Fortune, capricious dame, withdraws at once
The goodly prospect, to his eyes presents
Her, whom his conscious soul abhorr'd, and fear'd.
Lo! pushing thro' the crowd, a meagre form,
With hasty step, and visage incompos'd!
Wildly she star'd; rage sparkled in her eyes,
And Poverty sat shrinking on her cheeks.

Yet thro' the cloud that hung upon her brows,
A faded lustre broke, that dimly shone
Shorn of its beams, the ruins of a face,
Impair'd by time, and shatter'd by misfortunes.
A froward babe hung at her flabby breast,
And tugg'd for life; but wept, with hideous moan,
His frustrate hopes, and unavailing pains.
Another o'er her bending shoulder peep'd,
Swaddled around with rags of various hue.
He kens his comrade-twin with envious eye,
As of his share defrauded; then amain
He also screams, and to his brother's cries,
In doleful concert joins his loud laments.
O dire effect of lawless love! O sting
Of Pleasure past! As when a full-freight ship,
Blest in a rich return of pearls or gold,
Or fragrant spice, or silks of costly dye,
Makes to the wish'd-for port with swelling sails,
And all her gaudy trim display'd; o'erjoy'd

The master smiles; but if from some small creek,
A lurking corsair the rich quarry spies,
With all her sails bears down upon her prey,
And peals of thunder from her hollow sides
Check his triumphant course; aghast he stands,
Stiffen'd with fear, unable to resist,
And impotent to fly; all his fond hopes
Are dash'd at once; nought now, alas! remains
But the sad choice of slavery, or death.
So far'd it with the hapless HOBBINOL,
In the full blaze of his triumphant joy
Surpris'd by her, whose dreadful face alone
Cou'd shake his stedfast soul. In vain he turns,
And shifts his place averse; she haunts him still,
And glares upon him, with her haggard eyes,
That fiercely spoke her wrongs. Words swell'd with sighs
At length burst forth, and thus she storms enrag'd.

"KNOW'ST

"Know'st thou not me? false man! not to
"know me
"Argues thyself unknowing of thyself,
"Puff'd up with pride, and bloated with success.
"Is injur'd Mopsa then so soon forgot?
"Thou knew'st me once, ah! woe is me! thou
"did'st.
"But if laborious days, and sleepless nights,
"If hunger, cold, contempt, and penury,
"Inseparable guests, have thus disguis'd
"Thy once belov'd, thy handmaid dear; if thine
"And Fortune's frowns have blasted all my charms;
"If here no roses grow, no lilies bloom,
"Nor rear their heads on this neglected face;
"If thro' the world I range a slighted shade,
"The ghost of what I was, forlorn, unknown;
"At least know these. See! this sweet-simp'ring
"babe,
"Dear image of thyself; see! how it sprunts

"With

"With joy at thy approach! see, how it gilds
"Its soft smooth face, with false paternal smiles!
"Native deceit, from thee, base man, deriv'd!
"Or view this other elf, in ev'ry art
"Of smiling fraud, in ev'ry treach'rous leer,
"The very HOBBINOL! Ah! cruel man!
"Wicked, ingrate! And cou'd'st thou then so soon,
"So soon forget that pleasing fatal night,
"When me beneath the flow'ry thorn surpriz'd,
"Thy artful wiles betray'd? Was there a star,
"By which thou didst not swear? Was there a curse,
"A plague on earth, thou didst not then invoke
"On that devoted head; if e'er thy heart
"Prov'd haggard to my love, if e'er thy hand
"Declin'd the nuptial bond? But, oh! too well,
"Too well, alas! my throbbing breast perceiv'd
"The black impending storm; the conscious moon
"Veil'd in a sable cloud her modest face,
"And boding owls proclaim'd the dire event.

"And yet I love thee.—Oh! cou'd'ſt thou behold
"That image dwelling in my heart! But why?
"Why waſte I here theſe unavailing tears?
"On this thy minion, on this tawdry thing,
"On this gay victim, thus with garlands crown'd,
"All, all my vengeance fall!—Ye lightnings blaſt
"That face accurs'd, the ſource of all my woe!
"Arm, arm, ye furies! arm; all Hell break looſe!
"While thus I lead you to my juſt revenge,
"And thus"—Up ſtarts th' aſtoniſh'd HOBBINOL
To ſave his better half. "Fly, fly, he cries,
"Fly, my dear life, the fiend's malicious rage."
Born on the wings of fear away ſhe bounds,
And in the neighb'ring village pants forlorn.
So the cours'd hare to the cloſe covert flies,
Still trembling, tho' ſecure. Poor HOBBINOL
More grievous ills attend, around him preſs
A multitude, with huge HERCULEAN clubs,
Terrific band! the royal mandate theſe

Inſulting

Infulting fhew: arrefted, and amaz'd,
Half dead he ftands; no friends dare interpofe,
But bow dejected to th' imperial fcroll.
Such is the force of law. While confcious fhame
Sits heavy on his brow, they view the wretch
To RHADAMANTH's auguft tribunal dragg'd.
Good RHADAMANTH! to ev'ry wanton clown
Severe, indulgent to himfelf alone.

F I N I S.

www.ingramcontent.com/pod-product-compliance
Lightning Source LLC
Chambersburg PA
CBHW020114030726
47498CB00006B/2097
* 9 7 8 3 7 4 4 7 1 8 3 4 9 *